UNITED STATES ENCYCLOPEDIAS

THE GOVERNMENT ENCYCLOPEDIA

BY CARLA MOONEY

Encyclopedias

An Imprint of Abdo Reference
abdobooks.com

TABLE OF CONTENTS

FOUNDING OF THE US GOVERNMENT

Fifty-six delegates signed the Declaration of Independence, the official document that announced the separation of the American colonies from Great Britain.

The foundation of the US government was formed during the American Revolution (1775–1783). The leaders of the American colonies designed a system of government to help the new country grow. The new government would give power to the people. It was a radical idea at the time. That's because many nations, including Great Britain, had a monarchy. This meant that a king or queen ruled the country.

TENSIONS RISE WITH GREAT BRITAIN

The 13 American colonies were part of the British Empire in the 1700s. The British king and Parliament governed the colonies from overseas. But the colonies were thousands of miles from

Great Britain. The colonists became used to making decisions for themselves.

Great Britain became involved in the French and Indian War (1754–1763) in North America. It was an expensive war. Great Britain decided to increase taxes on the colonies to help cover the costs. Britain passed a series of unpopular laws and taxes. These included the Sugar Act, the Stamp Act, and the Intolerable Acts.

The American colonies resisted the new taxes. They were unhappy with British control over the colonies. The colonists

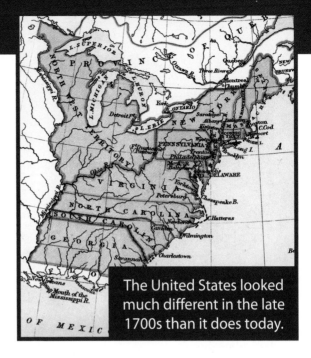

The United States looked much different in the late 1700s than it does today.

Great Britain and France fought over land in North America during the French and Indian War. Each nation had American Indian allies.

In 1773, colonists protested the British tax on tea by dumping chests of tea into Boston Harbor in Massachusetts. This event became known as the Boston Tea Party.

argued that they should have the same rights as British citizens living in Great Britain. This included the right to have representation in Parliament, the British lawmaking body. The colonists argued it was unfair to pay taxes without a voice in government. They called for "no taxation without representation." Britain dismissed their concerns. The British government said that the colonies already had virtual representation. This was the idea that Parliament represented the interests of all British subjects, including the colonists. Britain said the colonies didn't need their own representatives.

Tensions rose between Great Britain and the colonies. Delegates from the colonies met in Philadelphia, Pennsylvania, for the First Continental Congress in 1774. They appealed to

King George III of Great Britain to make peace with the colonies. Armed conflict broke out between British soldiers and the Massachusetts militia. They clashed in the cities of Lexington and Concord in April 1775. This marked the beginning of the American Revolution.

Delegates from all the colonies met in Philadelphia again in May 1775. This meeting was the Second Continental Congress. The Second Continental Congress approved the formation

Amid protests and high tensions, British soldiers killed five colonists during the Boston Massacre in 1770. This event made anti-British feelings in the colonies even stronger.

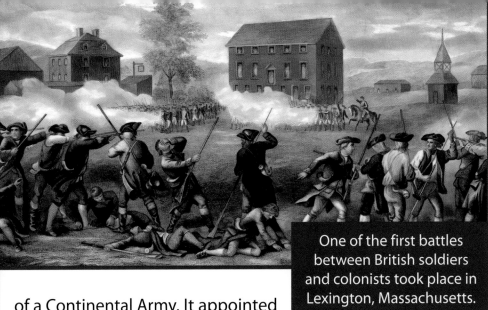

One of the first battles between British soldiers and colonists took place in Lexington, Massachusetts.

of a Continental Army. It appointed George Washington as the army commander. But some of the delegates and colonists wanted to avoid a war. They sent King George III the Olive Branch Petition. The petition asked King George III to make peace with the colonies. But he refused to even read it.

George Washington, *center*, had little experience leading large armies before becoming commander of the Continental Army.

Thomas Paine was one of the most influential writers during the American Revolution.

COMMON SENSE

Thomas Paine published a pamphlet titled *Common Sense* in January 1776. It was the first document that openly called for independence from Great Britain. Paine argued that the colonies should challenge the British government. He believed that a government should listen to its

JOIN, or DIE.

people and serve their needs. Britain had failed to do this. Paine wrote that the colonies should not have to be loyal to a country that treated them poorly. He called for the formation of a new nation.

Paine wrote his arguments in easy-to-understand language. *Common Sense* sold about 120,000 copies within a few months. By the end of the American Revolution, 500,000 copies had been sold. The pamphlet influenced many colonists and increased support for independence.

THE DECLARATION OF INDEPENDENCE

Richard Henry Lee of Virginia presented a resolution to the Second Continental Congress in June 1776. It called for the

Richard Henry Lee was involved in US politics from the American Revolution until 1792.

colonies to cut their ties with Great Britain. The colonies would then become "free and independent states." The delegates debated the resolution. They formed a committee to write a formal declaration of independence. This committee included Benjamin Franklin, John Adams, Thomas Jefferson, and others. The committee members discussed what should be included. They chose Thomas Jefferson to write the document.

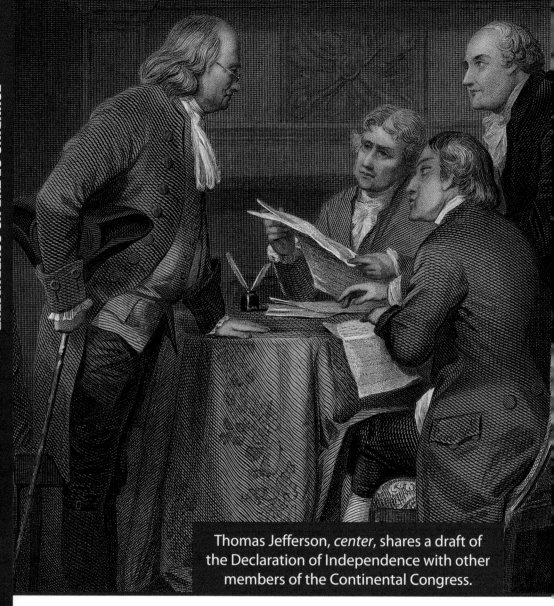

Thomas Jefferson, *center*, shares a draft of the Declaration of Independence with other members of the Continental Congress.

Jefferson produced the Declaration of Independence. This was the formal version of Lee's resolution. It announced the separation of the 13 American colonies from Great Britain. It explained the reasons why the colonies wanted independence. The Second Continental Congress approved the Declaration of Independence on July 4, 1776.

Delegates from all 13 colonies signed the Declaration of Independence.

The Articles of Confederation were adopted at Independence Hall in Philadelphia. The Declaration of Independence was also signed there.

ARTICLES OF CONFEDERATION

The American colonies had declared their independence from Great Britain. But they did not yet have a central government. The Second Continental Congress worked to design a government as the American Revolution continued. It drafted the Articles of Confederation in 1776. It declared the new country would be named the United States of America. Congress approved the Articles of Confederation in November 1777. The 13 states ratified the Articles. The document became the first US constitution on March 1, 1781.

ARTICLES

OF

Confederation

AND

Perpetual Union

BETWEEN THE

STATES

OF

NEW-HAMPSHIRE, MASSACHUSETTS-BAY, RHODE-ISLAND AND PROVIDENCE PLANTATIONS, CONNECTICUT, NEW-YORK, NEW-JERSEY, PENNSYLVANIA, DELAWARE, MARYLAND, VIRGINIA, NORTH-CAROLINA, SOUTH-CAROLINA AND GEORGIA.

LANCASTER:

PRINTED BY FRANCIS BAILEY.

M,DCC,LXXVII.

In 1777, Virginia was the first state to ratify the Articles of Confederation. Maryland ratified the document in 1781, the last state to do so.

The Second Continental Congress adopted a national flag in 1777.
The 13 stripes and stars represented each of the colonies.

The Articles of Confederation created a unicameral, or
single-house, legislature. This was Congress. It had the power
to declare war and appoint military officers. It could also make
alliances, sign treaties, and appoint foreign ambassadors.
Each state had equal representation in Congress. Nine of the
13 states had to approve a law for it to pass.

The Articles of Confederation established a loose union
among the states. Congress was hesitant to create a powerful
central government. It did not want the new government to
function like the British government. Most power was given
to the states. The Articles gave Congress the power to raise
money by asking the states for funding. But only the states
had the power to tax. Congress was not able to draft soldiers.
It could not regulate trade between the states. The Articles
did not establish a national court system or a president.

Delegates were limited to terms of no more than three years within any six-year period.

The Articles of Confederation intentionally created a weak central government. But the government was too weak to be effective. It could not pay for a strong military. It could not raise money to pay off debts from the American Revolution. Each state had different trading policies and currencies. This made it difficult for the states to trade with each other and with other countries.

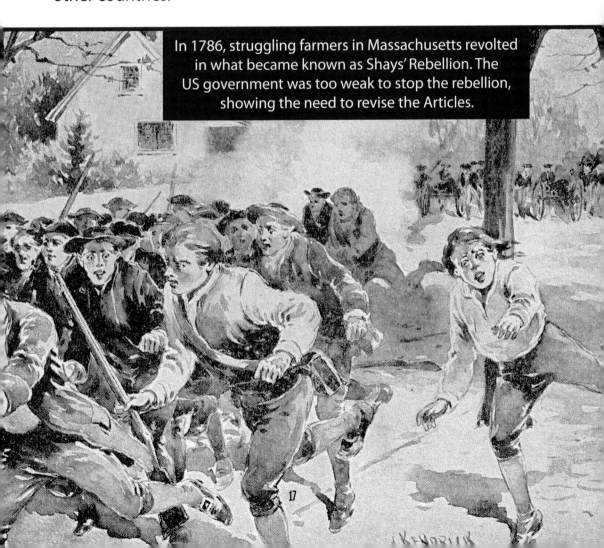

In 1786, struggling farmers in Massachusetts revolted in what became known as Shays' Rebellion. The US government was too weak to stop the rebellion, showing the need to revise the Articles.

CREATING A NEW CONSTITUTION

In 1787, leaders called for delegates to revise the Articles of Confederation. Twelve states sent delegates to the Constitutional Convention in Philadelphia. Only Rhode Island did not send a delegate. The delegates became known as the Founding Fathers. The delegates elected George Washington to lead the convention in a unanimous vote.

Unlike today, the US government and states each had their own currencies in the 1770s and 1780s.

Fifty-five delegates participated in the Constitutional Convention. They spent about three months debating and developing a new system of government.

The Founding Fathers realized that the Articles had many weaknesses. They decided that an entirely new document was needed. They hoped to create a stronger central government. They believed a new constitution could unify the states.

James Madison was a delegate from Virginia. He proposed an idea called the Virginia Plan. This plan called for a government system with three branches. A legislative branch would make laws. An executive branch would carry out laws. A judicial branch would interpret laws and determine if they were carried out fairly.

Congress would be a bicameral, or two-house, system under the Virginia Plan. The number of representatives in both houses would be determined by the state's population. Under this proposal, states with larger populations would have more representatives than states with smaller populations.

The Virginia Plan called for three branches of government. Because each branch would have different responsibilities, power would be balanced.

The presidential power to veto and other governmental powers were first outlined in the Virginia Plan.

The Virginia Plan also proposed a strong central government. It gave the central government the power to resolve disputes between the states. The people would not elect the president and the federal judges. They would be chosen by the legislative branch. The Virginia Plan also allowed the president to veto, or reject, laws passed by Congress. The two legislative houses could override the president's veto with enough votes.

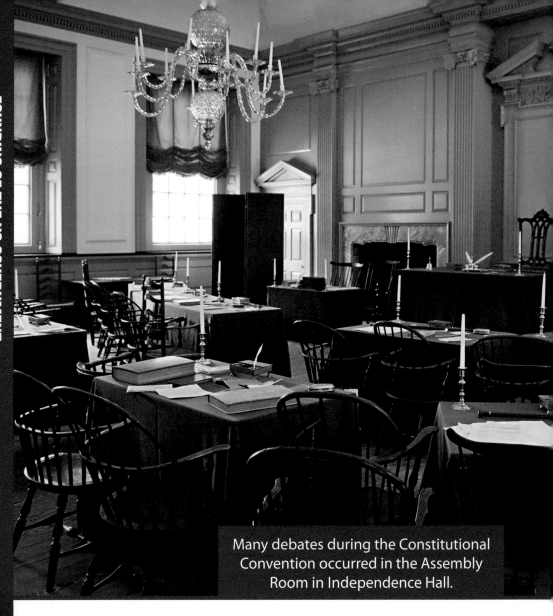

Many debates during the Constitutional Convention occurred in the Assembly Room in Independence Hall.

Most states with larger populations supported the Virginia Plan. Less-populated states opposed it. Smaller states would have little voice in the country's decisions and laws under this plan.

Delegates from New Jersey proposed a new idea as the debate continued. The New Jersey Plan also included a central

government with three branches. But it called for a unicameral legislature. The New Jersey Plan proposed for each state to have one vote in the legislature. This was similar to the Articles of Confederation. States with larger populations did not like the idea of each state having only one vote. They thought they needed more votes to reflect their larger populations. The New Jersey Plan had more support from states with smaller populations. It called for a weaker central government than the Virginia Plan. Much of the power would still remain with the states. But the central government would be able to tax and regulate trade among states.

William Paterson was the delegate who proposed the New Jersey Plan.

COMPROMISES TO THE CONSTITUTION

Debate over the Virginia Plan and the New Jersey Plan went on for weeks. The Constitutional Convention came up with the Great Compromise. It decided that the legislature would be bicameral. Each state would have two members in the upper house. This would be the Senate. This part of the proposal was like the New Jersey Plan. A state's population would determine the number of representatives it had in the lower house. This would be the House of Representatives. This part was similar to the Virginia Plan. The delegates approved the Great Compromise on July 16, 1787.

Connecticut delegates Roger Sherman and Oliver Ellsworth proposed the Great Compromise in 1787.

Many enslaved people were forced to work on plantations in the southern states.

Next the Founding Fathers had to decide how to count state populations. This would help them divide the spots in the House of Representatives between states. It also affected the amount of money each state would owe the national government in taxes.

The southern states relied on the work of enslaved people to grow crops. They wanted to count enslaved workers as

The Liberty Bell is a symbol of the efforts to end slavery.

part of the population for representatives. The southern states had more people than the northern states. However, most of that population was made up of enslaved people. The southern states would have fewer representatives than the northern states if only free white men were counted. But the southern states did not want to include enslaved people as part of their populations when determining taxes. This would allow them to pay less money in taxes. The northern states had the opposite view. They wanted enslaved people to be counted for taxes but not for representatives.

The delegates debated the issue. They came up with the Three-Fifths Compromise. Three-fifths of the state's population of enslaved people would count toward the state's total population. This number would affect both representation and taxation. Enslaved people were not given the right to vote.

The delegates also debated a ban on the slave trade. They agreed to give Congress the power to ban the import of

By the time Abraham Lincoln, *left*, issued the Emancipation Proclamation in 1863 to free enslaved people, many northern states had already banned slavery.

The bald eagle became a national symbol for the United States in 1789.

enslaved people. This ban would not go into effect for 20 years. The United States did not formally ban the international slave trade until 1808.

A NEW PLAN, A NEW CONSTITUTION

Choosing a new plan of government for the United States took four months. After the debates, the Founding Fathers wrote the US Constitution. It included the principles of the US government. It also included political compromises. The majority of the delegates signed the Constitution on September 17, 1787. They hoped the new Constitution would strengthen the young country.

This painting from the 1800s shows Betsy Ross, *left*, sewing the first US flag, which had 13 stars. However, historians say there isn't evidence that Ross designed the flag herself.

Alexander Hamilton was born in the British West Indies. He arrived in the American colonies in 1772. He fought in the American Revolution. Hamilton believed in a strong central government. He wrote an address in 1786 that called for a convention to revise the Articles of Confederation. This led to the Constitutional Convention in 1787.

Hamilton was one of the authors of the Federalist Papers that helped increase support for the Constitution. He served as the first US secretary of the treasury. He helped establish rules and policies about how the United States handled money. He also

Alexander Hamilton was killed in a duel on July 12, 1804.

suggested creating a national bank. Hamilton helped set up a financial plan to manage the country's debt from the American Revolution. He built credit for the government. Hamilton set up the US Mint and created a system for international trade. These policies increased the power of the federal government. Some of Hamilton's opponents, including Thomas Jefferson, thought the states should have more power. This debate eventually led to the rise of political parties in the United States.

Hamilton is featured on the US ten-dollar bill.

The Constitution needed to be ratified by nine of the 13 states to become official. But some states were opposed to the Constitution. They did not like the idea of a strong central government. Alexander Hamilton, James Madison, and John Jay wrote the Federalist Papers to convince people to support the Constitution. This series of 85 essays pointed out the weaknesses of the Articles of Confederation. They argued that the Constitution would fix these problems while still protecting peoples' freedom.

FEDERALIST VS. ANTI-FEDERALIST

Two sides developed as the Founding Fathers drafted the Constitution. One side was known as the Federalists. Federalists supported the Constitution and wanted a strong national government. The other side was called the Anti-Federalists. They opposed the Constitution. They wanted the states to have more power. Both Federalists and Anti-Federalists wanted to protect individual rights and freedoms. They disagreed over whether a strong national government was the best way to protect those freedoms.

On December 7, 1787, Delaware became the first state to ratify the Constitution. Pennsylvania, New Jersey, Georgia, and Connecticut soon followed. Some states refused to ratify the Constitution unless it included protections for individual rights. Massachusetts ratified the Constitution in 1788 under the condition that such amendments would be added. Six other states followed Massachusetts's example. New Hampshire became the ninth state to ratify the Constitution on June 21, 1788. This made the Constitution the official framework for the US government.

THE

FEDERALIST:

A COLLECTION

OF

E S S A Y S,

WRITTEN IN FAVOUR OF THE

NEW CONSTITUTION,

AS AGREED UPON BY THE FEDERAL CONVENTION,
SEPTEMBER 17, 1787.

IN TWO VOLUMES.

VOL. I.

N E W - Y O R K:

PRINTED AND SOLD BY J. AND A. M'LEAN,
No. 41, HANOVER-SQUARE.

The authors of the Federalist Papers did not include their names when they published the essays in New York newspapers.

THE CONSTITUTION AND THE BILL OF RIGHTS

The Founding Fathers drafted the Constitution in 116 days.

The Founding Fathers laid out the framework for the US government in the Constitution. This document defined the fundamental rights of US citizens. Changes have been made to the Constitution over time. But the United States has followed these principles of government for more than 200 years. This makes the US Constitution the oldest written national constitution still in use today.

REPRESENTATIVE VS. DIRECT DEMOCRACY

The Constitution established the United States as a representative democracy. Citizens elect officials to represent them in this form of government. These officials work to pass laws that represent the values of the voters. A representative democracy differs from a direct democracy. Citizens vote directly on laws in a direct democracy. They make all governmental decisions themselves.

US representatives are meant to uphold the ideals of the voters who elected them.

The Founding Fathers worried about giving the people too much power. They thought elected officials would be better at making wise decisions. The Founding Fathers also believed that a representative democracy would protect minority opinions. It would be difficult for a minority population to make political changes in a direct democracy.

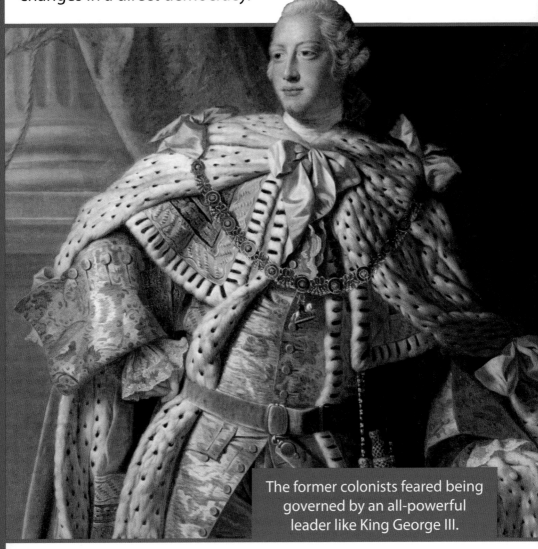

The former colonists feared being governed by an all-powerful leader like King George III.

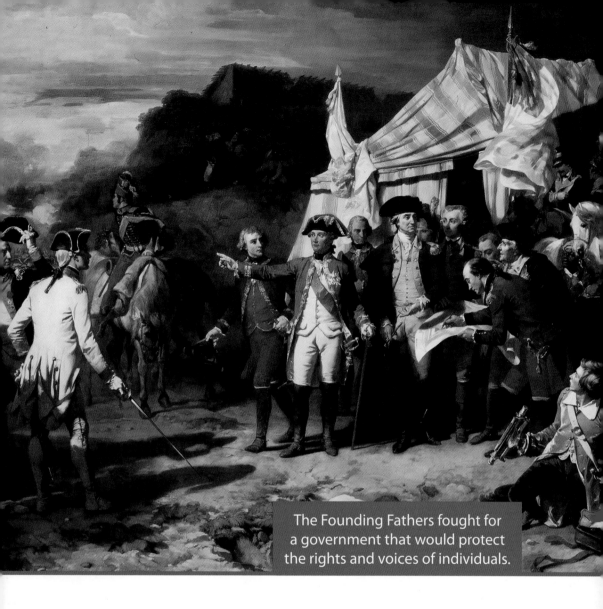

The Founding Fathers fought for a government that would protect the rights and voices of individuals.

The US government is also a constitutional democracy. This means the Constitution itself limits the power of the government. The Founding Fathers recognized that a king with unchecked power threatened people's rights. The Founders worried that those in power could prevent their opponents from running for election in the future. The Constitution allows the minority to speak out against the majority.

The Constitution calls for the free and fair election of government officials. This means elections are held regularly. Voters each receive one vote. They can vote for the candidate of their choice. They do not feel pressured to vote for a candidate

The US Constitution is on display in the National Archives building.

they do not like. Voting polls are monitored and ballots are counted to help prevent election fraud. Free and fair elections ensure that there is a peaceful transfer of power.

James Madison was born on March 16, 1751. He was appointed to the Virginia Convention in 1776. Madison was one of the authors of the Virginia Constitution. He later served as a delegate in the First Continental Congress.

Madison represented Virginia at the Constitutional Convention. He proposed the Virginia Plan. This plan called for states with larger populations to receive more

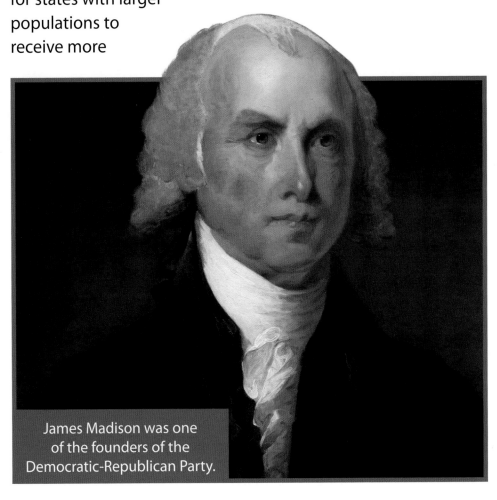

James Madison was one of the founders of the Democratic-Republican Party.

James Madison's home in Montpelier Station, Virginia, is now a museum where visitors can learn about US history and the Constitution.

representation in Congress. This idea and many other suggestions made by Madison were included in the final draft of the Constitution. Madison is nicknamed the Father of the Constitution for his role in writing the document.

Madison also played a major role in the ratification process. He helped provide the framework for the Bill of Rights. He also was one of the main authors of the Federalist Papers, along with Alexander Hamilton and John Jay.

In 1809, Madison became the fourth president of the United States. He served for two terms. Madison died on June 28, 1836.

The US government is responsible for protecting all US citizens.

WHAT DOES THE CONSTITUTION SAY?

The Constitution begins with a statement called a preamble. The preamble describes the intent of the US government. It states, "We the people of the United States, in order to form a more perfect Union, establish justice, ensure domestic tranquility, provide for the common defense . . . do ordain and establish this Constitution for the United States of America." The words "We the people" show that the country would be ruled by the people. The nation would not be ruled by a king, queen, or president.

Seven articles follow the preamble. They describe the organization and responsibilities of the government. The first three articles establish the three branches of government. They are the legislative, executive, and judicial branches. These articles also describe the powers of these branches.

Senator Oliver Ellsworth was the primary author of the Judiciary Act of 1789 that set up the federal court system.

Article I details the legislative branch, Congress. It gives Congress the authority and responsibility to make laws.

Article II establishes the executive branch. This includes the offices of the president and vice president. It details the rules for electing a president. Article II also describes the requirements a person needs to become president.

Article III forms the judicial branch. It establishes the US Supreme Court as the highest court in the country.

This article states that federal judges and Supreme Court justices are appointed for life. Article III establishes only the basic framework for the court system. The details were left for Congress to determine later.

The remaining four articles of the Constitution detail ways to balance federal power and change the Constitution. Article IV gives states the power to create and enforce their own laws. Article IV also prevents the US government from discriminating against states. It cannot pass laws that will affect some states more than the others. Article IV also details the process for adding new states.

Congress proposed the Equal Rights Amendment to prevent discrimination based on sex in 1972. But it was not passed by three-fourths of the states before the time limit passed.

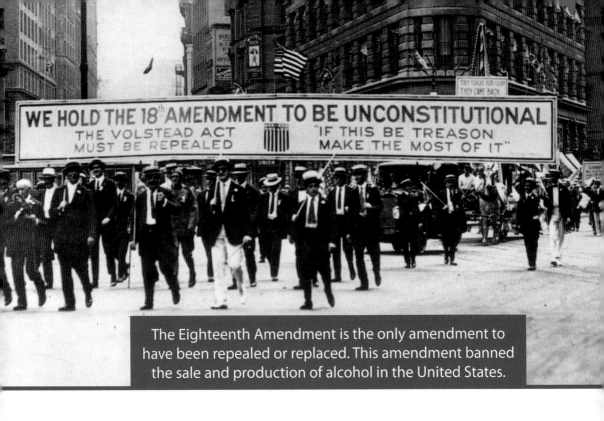

WE HOLD THE 18ᵗʰ AMENDMENT TO BE UNCONSTITUTIONAL

THE VOLSTEAD ACT
MUST BE REPEALED

"IF THIS BE TREASON
MAKE THE MOST OF IT"

The Eighteenth Amendment is the only amendment to have been repealed or replaced. This amendment banned the sale and production of alcohol in the United States.

Article V describes the process for amending, or changing, the Constitution. The Founding Fathers recognized that there might be a need to make changes to the Constitution. They created a way to make these changes, called amendments. The Founders wanted the amendment process to be difficult. This would give stability to the new government.

There are two main steps in the amendment process. First, an amendment must be approved for proposal to the states. There are two ways for this to happen. Two-thirds of each house of Congress must agree to propose the amendment to the states. In the second way, the states propose an amendment themselves. Two-thirds of the states must request the amendment for it to move forward. This method has never been used. After the amendment has been proposed, it must be ratified by three-fourths of the states.

Approximately 11,850 amendments have been proposed in Congress between 1789 and 2019. Only 33 have received the two-thirds votes in Congress and were sent to the states for ratification. Just 27 amendments, including the ten in the Bill of Rights, have been ratified by the states.

Article VI establishes that federal law is higher than state and local laws. It is

STATE AND LOCAL GOVERNMENTS

Each US state and local jurisdiction has its own government. The Constitution requires all states to have a republican form of government. This means the power belongs to citizens. The three-branch system is not required. However, all US state governments have an executive, legislative, and judicial branch.

New York City celebrated the ratification of the Constitution on July 26, 1788.

unlawful for states to pass laws that go against federal law. Article VII describes the ratification process for the Constitution. It required nine states to ratify the Constitution for it to become law. All 13 states ratified the Constitution. Rhode Island ratified the document on May 29, 1790. It was the last state to do so.

CHECKS AND BALANCES

The Constitution created a strong federal government. The Founding Fathers wanted to ensure that the government would not become too powerful. This is why they separated the government's powers into three branches. Different branches have different responsibilities. Federal power would not be concentrated in a single branch.

Supreme Court justices are nominated by the president. These nominations are then reviewed by Congress.

The Founders also created a system of checks and balances. This made sure that an individual branch would not become too powerful. Each branch can check and limit the power of the other branches. For example, Congress may pass a bill. It must be signed by the president before it becomes a law. This prevents the legislative branch from using too much power. Congress also keeps presidential powers in check. The president has the power to veto a bill. Congress can override that veto with a two-thirds vote in both houses.

The House exercised its power to check the presidency when it impeached Donald Trump. Trump was acquitted by the Senate in February 2020.

John Marshall was chief justice of the Supreme Court during *Marbury v. Madison*, which gave the Court the power to declare a law unconstitutional.

Congress has the power to impeach the president and other federal officials. Impeachment is when Congress charges a government official with a serious crime. If the official is convicted, or found guilty, that person could be removed from office. The official could also be banned from running for office in the future.

The judicial branch can check the powers of the other two branches. It has the power to strike down a law that does not

Training soldiers in the US Army is a responsibility of the federal government that is described in the Constitution.

follow the Constitution. The judicial branch can also remove a presidential act that is unconstitutional.

FEDERAL VS. STATE POWERS

The Constitution gives three types of power to the federal government. These are delegated powers, implied powers, and inherent powers. Delegated powers are listed in the Constitution. These powers include the ability to print money, create an army, regulate commerce, and declare war. The Constitution lists 27 delegated powers for the federal government.

Implied powers are not explicitly defined in the Constitution. They fall under a clause in Article I that gives

Congress the right "to make all laws which shall be necessary and proper." The creation of a national bank was an example of an implied power. The Constitution does not mention a power to create a banking system. But the first US secretary of the treasury, Alexander Hamilton, believed it was necessary in order to build the US economy.

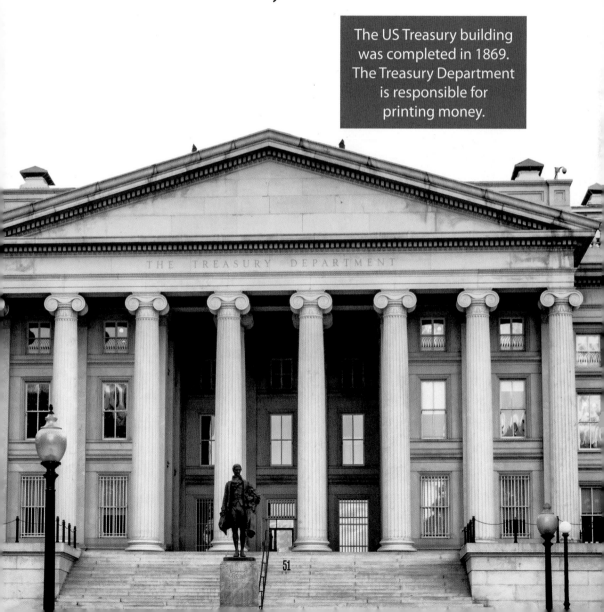

The US Treasury building was completed in 1869. The Treasury Department is responsible for printing money.

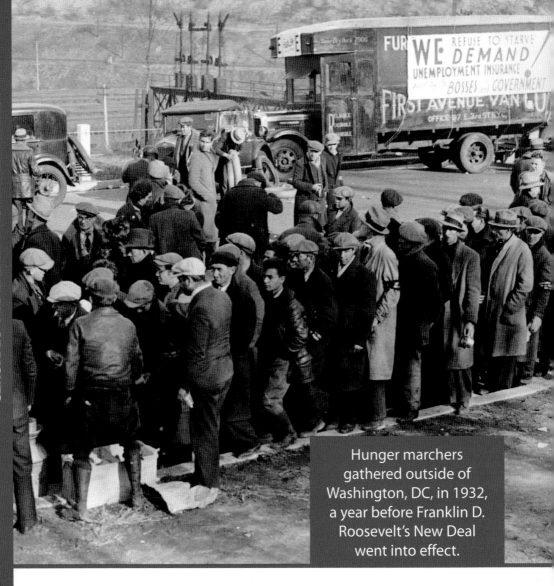

Hunger marchers gathered outside of Washington, DC, in 1932, a year before Franklin D. Roosevelt's New Deal went into effect.

Inherent power is also not explicitly listed in the Constitution. The first three articles of the Constitution have a Vesting Clause that gives inherent powers to the branches of government. Inherent powers allow the government to respond quickly to emergencies. For example, Franklin D. Roosevelt was president during an economic downturn known as the Great Depression. He used inherent power to pass policies to provide economic relief.

The Constitution grants certain powers to the federal government. It also reserves some powers for the states. Reserved powers are guaranteed in the Tenth Amendment. They include establishing local governments, conducting elections, and regulating trade within the state.

The Constitution also prohibits some powers. The federal government cannot interfere with a state's ability to perform its duties. States are prohibited from taxing imports and exports. They also are not allowed to create their own currency.

Having a standard national currency makes it easier to purchase goods from other nations.

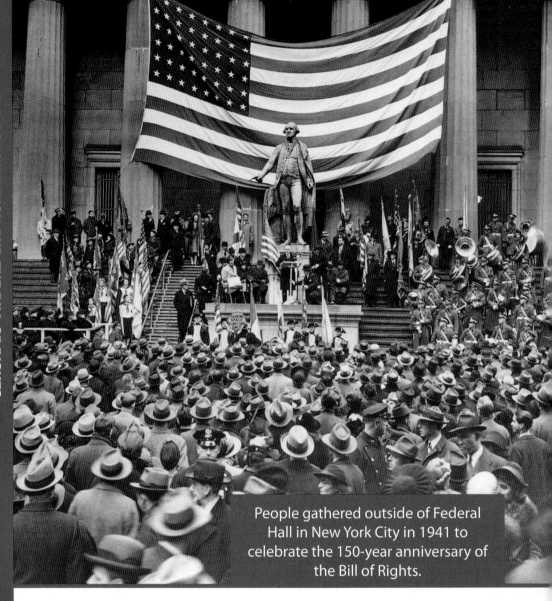

People gathered outside of Federal Hall in New York City in 1941 to celebrate the 150-year anniversary of the Bill of Rights.

BILL OF RIGHTS

In 1789, many Americans worried that the Constitution would not protect individual rights. That year, Congress responded to those concerns by proposing a list of twelve amendments. The states ratified ten of the twelve amendments in 1791. These first ten amendments became known as the Bill of Rights.

The Bill of Rights was a necessary addition for some states. They were not willing to ratify the Constitution unless the Bill of Rights was included. The Constitution created a strong government. The Bill of Rights made sure the government could not take away individual rights. It prevented the US government from acting as the British monarchy had during the colonial period.

Members of the military are chosen to watch over the original drafts of the Bill of Rights, Constitution, and Declaration of Independence.

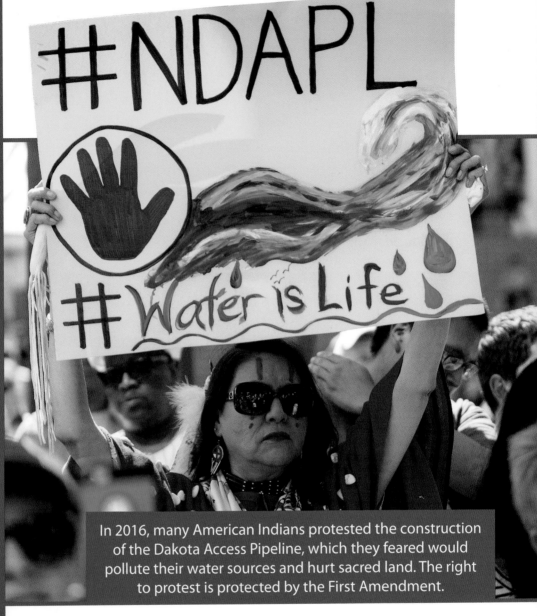

In 2016, many American Indians protested the construction of the Dakota Access Pipeline, which they feared would pollute their water sources and hurt sacred land. The right to protest is protected by the First Amendment.

The First Amendment is one of the most well-known amendments. It protects five fundamental freedoms. These include freedom of religion, freedom of speech, and freedom of the press. It also gives individuals the freedom of assembly and freedom to petition the government. This allows citizens to protest and criticize the government.

Protesters in Springfield, Massachusetts, gathered in support of gun law reform. Others protested against these policies, as they believe strict gun laws violate the Second Amendment.

Many citizens feared abuse from a professional army. The Second and Third Amendments were created to defend against this. The Second Amendment guarantees Americans the right to bear arms and serve in a state militia. People would be able to protect themselves if the government became too powerful. The Third Amendment has its roots in the colonial period. The colonists were sometimes forced to house British soldiers. The Third Amendment says people cannot be forced to house US soldiers. The Fourth Amendment protects people's privacy. It prevents unreasonable searches and seizures.

A jury listens to each side of a case and determines whether a person is guilty or not guilty.

The Fifth Amendment guarantees certain rights to people accused of crimes. For example, a person cannot be tried for a serious crime without being charged by a grand jury. This is called due process. This amendment protects a person from being tried more than once for the same crime. It also states that people cannot be forced to testify against themselves.

The Sixth, Seventh, and Eighth Amendments guarantee additional rights to people accused of crimes. The Sixth Amendment guarantees the right to a fair and speedy trial. It states that an accused person has the right to a lawyer. An accused person also has the right to call upon witnesses to

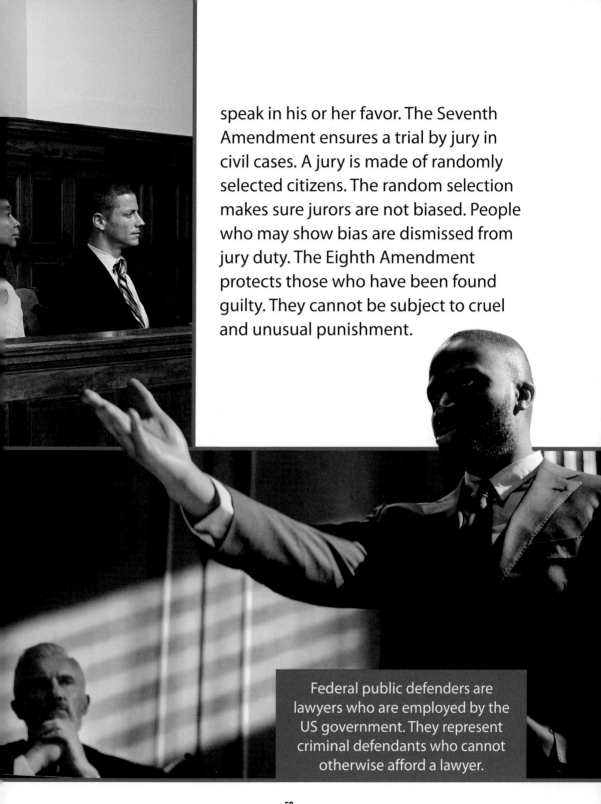

speak in his or her favor. The Seventh Amendment ensures a trial by jury in civil cases. A jury is made of randomly selected citizens. The random selection makes sure jurors are not biased. People who may show bias are dismissed from jury duty. The Eighth Amendment protects those who have been found guilty. They cannot be subject to cruel and unusual punishment.

Federal public defenders are lawyers who are employed by the US government. They represent criminal defendants who cannot otherwise afford a lawyer.

The Ninth Amendment states that the rights listed in the Constitution are not the only rights of the American people. The Tenth Amendment further protects individual rights. It declares that any powers not mentioned in the Constitution remain with the states or the people.

IMPORTANT AMENDMENTS

The Bill of Rights and several other amendments have expanded individual freedoms. They have adjusted the role of the federal government. Southern states left the Union during the American Civil War (1861–1865). They formed the Confederate States of America. Confederate states wanted to create a new government in which slavery would remain legal. The Union won the war. Slavery was outlawed.

People who protested against COVID-19 vaccine mandates sometimes cited the Ninth Amendment. They argued this amendment gave them the right to choose what went into their bodies.

President Abraham Lincoln, *second from left*, reads a draft of the Emancipation Proclamation to his cabinet members. This document freed enslaved people in the United States.

A LONG TIME TO RATIFICATION

Since the early 1900s, Congress has given the states a time limit of seven years to ratify an amendment. The amendment dies if it is not ratified within that time frame. Congress has the authority to extend the time limit. The Twenty-Seventh Amendment was proposed in 1789 as one of the original 12 amendments. It stated that Congress could not pass immediate pay raises for its members. The amendment was not ratified with the Bill of Rights. But Congress had not set a time limit for the ratification. The amendment was eventually ratified in 1992.

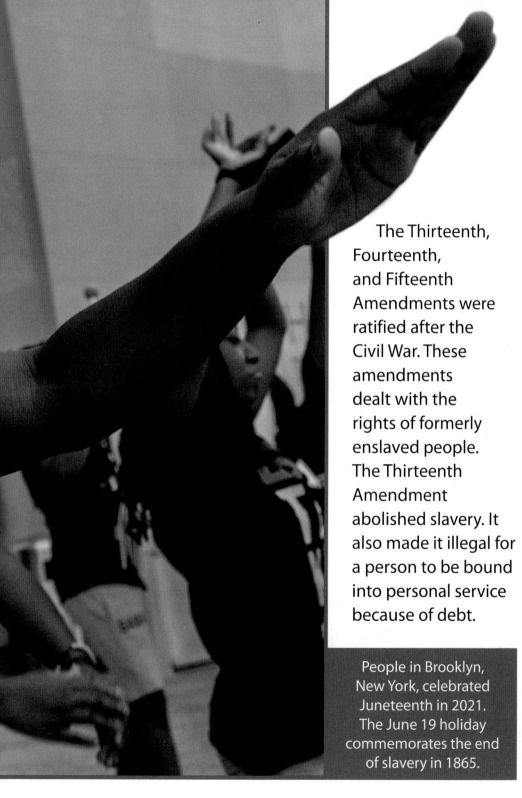

The Thirteenth, Fourteenth, and Fifteenth Amendments were ratified after the Civil War. These amendments dealt with the rights of formerly enslaved people. The Thirteenth Amendment abolished slavery. It also made it illegal for a person to be bound into personal service because of debt.

People in Brooklyn, New York, celebrated Juneteenth in 2021. The June 19 holiday commemorates the end of slavery in 1865.

The Fourteenth Amendment includes the Equal Protection Clause. This guarantees that all people are entitled to equal protection under the law. It granted US citizenship and due process for formerly enslaved people. It defined citizenship as a right given to all people born in the United States. But American Indians and immigrants still struggled to earn citizenship for many years.

Water fountains in some states were segregated until 1954, when the Supreme Court ruled that segregation was unconstitutional.

PAY YOUR POLL TAX - NOW!

Deadline January 31st

Vote! And Protect Your Rights and Privileges

Be Ready For Every Election---

Local Option and Other Special Elections are in Prospect for This Year

Black Americans still faced barriers to voting after the ratification of the Fifteenth Amendment. Poll taxes prevented many formerly enslaved people from voting because they could not afford the fee.

The Fourteenth Amendment was ratified in 1868. It has been used in the fight for equal rights in the United States. For example, Southern states separated Black people and white people after the Civil War. This process was called segregation. Black people had to go to different schools and use different facilities than white people. This changed after the 1954 Supreme Court case *Brown v. Board of Education*. The Supreme Court said that segregation went against the Equal Protection Clause in the Fourteenth Amendment.

The Fifteenth Amendment establishes penalties if a state denies citizens the right to vote. It also bans public officials

Franklin D. Roosevelt served as president from 1933 to 1945, leading the United States during the Great Depression and World War II (1939–1945).

who have encouraged rebellion from holding office. This prevented former Confederate leaders from working in the

US government. The amendment also denied federal funding to pay the Confederacy's war debts. Former slaveholders could not collect money as repayment for the loss of their enslaved workers.

Another major change to the Constitution came in the Twenty-Second Amendment. The Constitution did not originally set a term limit for presidents. Franklin D. Roosevelt was the only US president to serve for more than two terms. He was elected to a fourth term in 1944. He died in office a year later. Congress passed the Twenty-Second Amendment after Roosevelt's death. This amendment limited the president to two four-year terms. It stated that someone can serve as president for a maximum of ten years. The vice president takes over as president if the president dies in office or resigns. He or she serves for the rest of the term. If the remainder of the term was two years or fewer, the person is eligible to run two more times. The states ratified this amendment in 1951.

EXECUTIVE BRANCH

The executive branch is one of the three branches of government. This branch carries out and enforces the country's laws. Some members of this branch have diplomatic responsibilities with other countries. The executive branch has more than 2,000 different agencies. It employs more than four million Americans. The president, vice president, cabinet members, and many others are part of the executive branch. The military is also part of this branch.

The president lives and works in the White House.

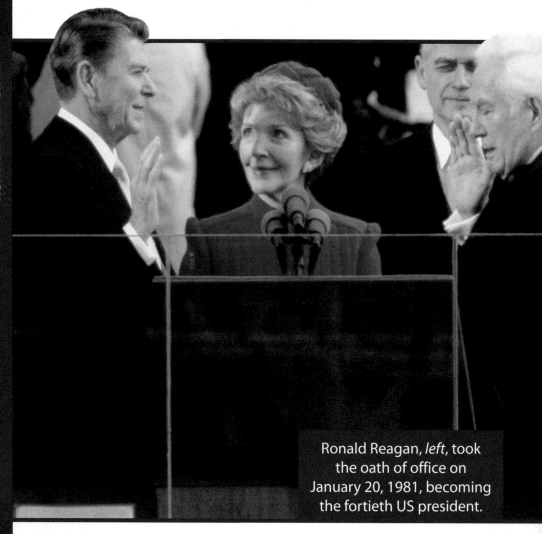

Ronald Reagan, *left*, took the oath of office on January 20, 1981, becoming the fortieth US president.

THE PRESIDENT

The president of the United States is the leader of the executive branch. He or she also serves as the country's head of state. The president is elected to a four-year term. The Constitution states that the president must meet three qualifications. To serve as president, a person must be at least 35 years of age. He or she must be a natural-born citizen. A presidential candidate needs to have lived in the United States for at least 14 years.

The Constitution grants the president several powers. The president serves as the commander in chief of the armed forces. He or she also negotiates treaties with other countries. The president appoints federal judges and other federal officers. The president also has the power to sign bills into law or veto them.

As commander in chief, the president has the power to authorize military actions.

Diplomacy is a presidential responsibility. Joe Biden and the United States hosted the Ninth Summit of the Americas in June 2022 to discuss trade and other issues with leaders from North and South America.

The president selects the members of the cabinet. Cabinet members are important advisors to the president. They head various executive departments. They report back to the president. This helps the president make informed decisions. For example, the secretary of education is a cabinet position. This cabinet member tells the president about the country's education system. Then the president can take steps to improve educational policies. The president also appoints the heads of more than 50 independent federal commissions, such as the Securities and Exchange Commission (SEC).

The president can issue executive orders. These are legally binding orders given to federal agencies. Executive orders usually tell officials how to apply a law or policy. But presidents have also used executive orders to act without Congressional approval. Some of these orders have had major effects on the country. Abraham Lincoln freed enslaved people with an executive order. Dwight D. Eisenhower issued an executive order to desegregate schools. Other presidents have used executive orders to enter wars. Some people worry that executive orders give presidents too much power.

President George W. Bush, *center*, held a press conference at the White House with his cabinet members in 2008.

The president also has the power to grant clemencies and pardons for federal crimes. Clemencies reduce a person's sentence. Pardons eliminate a sentence entirely. As with executive orders, some people feel that these abilities give the president too much power. For example, Andrew Johnson pardoned more than 13,000 people during his time as president. Some of the pardons included Confederate officials.

President Gerald Ford, *pictured*, pardoned former president Richard Nixon of crimes related to a political scandal in 1974. Today historians believe the pardon allowed the government to focus on more pressing issues.

Barack Obama delivered his final State of the Union Address before Congress on January 12, 2016. Obama was the first Black president of the United States.

The Constitution describes several presidential responsibilities. One is to give Congress updates on how the country is doing. This is traditionally done in a speech called the State of the Union address. The president speaks about the country's current condition. The speech celebrates the administration's accomplishments and describes future plans.

George Washington was born in February 1732. He was the head of the Constitutional Convention in 1787. When state electors met to choose the first president in 1789, they all selected Washington. He was the only president to be chosen unanimously.

Washington had many accomplishments as president.

George Washington served in the French and Indian War and the American Revolution before becoming the first US president.

Washington created a plan to reduce national debt along with his secretary of the treasury, Alexander Hamilton. He also moved the nation's capital from New York City to a new district that would become Washington, DC. France and Great Britain went to war during Washington's presidency. Hamilton advised Washington to side with the British. Thomas Jefferson, Washington's secretary of state, suggested allying with the

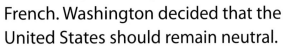

French. Washington decided that the United States should remain neutral.

Washington hoped to keep the government united. He disagreed with the formation of political parties. He did not want lawmakers to feel bound to the party when making political decisions. But political parties began to develop during Washington's presidency. Federalists supported a strong federal government. Democratic-Republicans believed more power should be kept with the states.

Washington served two terms as president. He retired to Mount Vernon, Virginia, in 1797. He died on December 14, 1799.

Kamala Harris was sworn in as Biden's vice president in January 2021. She became the first female vice president in US history.

THE VICE PRESIDENT

The vice president is part of the executive branch. This position is directly under the president. The vice president is first in the line of succession. The line of succession is the order in which federal officials take over the presidency if needed. The vice president takes over if the president dies, resigns, or becomes unable to perform presidential duties.

Dick Cheney, *left*, was vice president to George W. Bush and had a major role in the administration's foreign policy in the Middle East. In 2008, Cheney met with the president of Palestine.

VICE PRESIDENT ELECTIONS

Presidents and vice presidents were elected separately in the first draft of the Constitution. The presidential candidate who received the most votes would become president. The runner-up would become the vice president. This meant the president and vice president could belong to different political parties. This made it difficult for the government to accomplish goals. The Twelfth Amendment changed this policy in 1804. After that, presidents were able to select their running mates.

The vice president and a majority of cabinet members can determine whether the president is unfit for office. They can decide to remove the president from office if they believe the president is unable to carry out presidential duties. This removal process begins within the executive branch. Another removal process is impeachment, which begins with Congress. Permanent removal of a president has not occurred. Ronald Reagan and George H. W. Bush both temporarily passed presidential power to their vice presidents as they underwent surgeries. Nine vice presidents have become president after the sitting president died or resigned.

Theodore Roosevelt became president after President William McKinley was killed while in office. Roosevelt won election to another term in 1904.

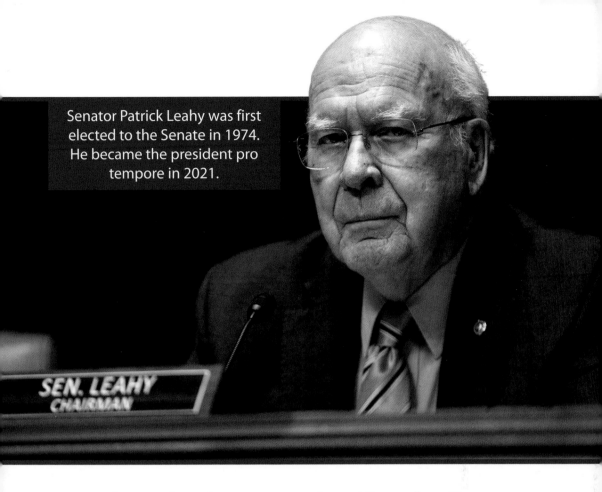
Senator Patrick Leahy was first elected to the Senate in 1974. He became the president pro tempore in 2021.

Presidents select their vice presidents. They take office at the same time. Vice presidents serve a four-year term. There is no limit to how many terms a vice president can serve. A vice president can serve under multiple presidents if selected to do so.

The vice president is the president of the US Senate. He or she casts the deciding vote if there is a tied vote among senators. But the vice president rarely presides over the Senate's everyday activities. The Senate instead selects one of its members as the president pro tempore. The person in this position signs legislation and issues the oath of office to new senators. He or she is in the line of succession.

THE EXECUTIVE OFFICE OF THE PRESIDENT

Franklin D. Roosevelt established the Executive Office of the President (EOP) in 1939. The EOP assists the president in making decisions and governing. The White House chief of staff oversees the EOP. The EOP handles many tasks. This includes managing presidential communications to the country and promoting trade overseas. The offices and number of advisors in the EOP can change as the president's needs change. The president's EOP can include thousands of individuals and many offices and councils.

The Senate must confirm nominees to some EOP roles. The president can appoint others without confirmation. The EOP includes the Office of the Press Secretary. The press secretary gives daily briefings to the media about the president's activities. The National Security Council is also part of the EOP.

James Hagerty served as White House press secretary under President Dwight D. Eisenhower from 1953 to 1961.

Lloyd J. Austin III was sworn in as secretary of defense in January 2021.

It provides the president with advice on foreign policy, national security, and more.

Other offices within the EOP maintain the White House. They manage the president's schedule and transportation. For example, the White House Military Office manages the aircraft that carry the president. It also oversees the White House dining facilities.

An airplane that is carrying the president is called Air Force One.

THE CABINET AND THE EXECUTIVE DEPARTMENTS

The cabinet is made up of 15 of the president's top advisors. The president appoints the cabinet members. Cabinet members need to be confirmed by a majority of senators. The EOP directly supports and responds to the president's needs. Cabinet members are more independent than the EOP. Each cabinet member leads a different department within the executive branch. These departments include the Departments of State, the Treasury, Defense, Homeland Security, the Interior, Agriculture, Commerce, Labor, Health and Human Services, Housing and Urban Development, Transportation, Education, Energy, and Veterans Affairs. The attorney general is also a cabinet member. The president can dismiss members of the cabinet at any time. Cabinet members are part of the line of succession.

The cabinet members and their departments are responsible for the operation of the federal government. Each department has a unique set of responsibilities. Deputies and assistant secretaries support the cabinet members. They lead

President Jimmy Carter, *second from right*, met with his cabinet members to discuss natural gas shortages in 1977.

Alberto R. Gonzales served as the US Attorney General from 2005 to 2007. He was the first Hispanic person to hold the position.

programs and initiatives of the department. Each department is typically divided into bureaus, divisions, and sections.

For example, the Secret Service is a federal law enforcement agency. It is a division of the Department of Homeland Security.

The Department of Defense (DOD) is the executive department with the most members. The DOD is headquartered at the Pentagon near Washington, DC. It recruits people to join US military forces and deters war by creating a strong military. The DOD provides aid and disaster relief nationally and internationally. It performs peacekeeping duties in the United States and around the world. The DOD includes military branches such as the Army, Navy, and Air Force. It also has other agencies and offices such as the National Security Agency and the Defense Intelligence Agency. The DOD employs more than 1.4 million military personnel on active duty. It also includes 700,000 civilian personnel and 1.1 million National Guard and Reserve forces.

DEPARTMENT OF HEALTH AND HUMAN SERVICES

The Department of Health and Human Services (HHS) is an executive department. Approximately 65,000 employees work in the HHS. They protect the health of Americans and provide essential human services. HHS divisions include the National Institutes of Health, the Food and Drug Administration, and the Centers for Disease Control and Prevention. These agencies perform medical research, monitor food and drug safety, and help prevent disease outbreaks. The HHS also administers Medicare and Medicaid. These programs provide health insurance for 25 percent of Americans.

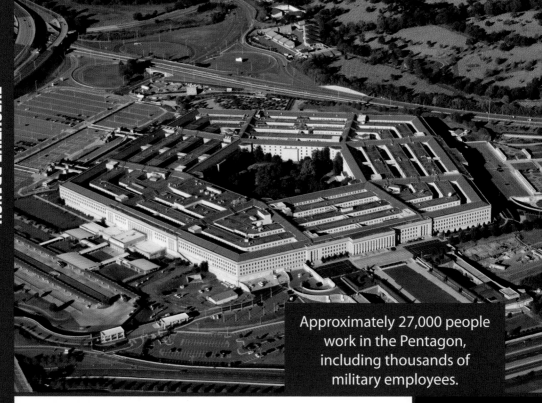

Approximately 27,000 people work in the Pentagon, including thousands of military employees.

INDEPENDENT AGENCIES

The executive branch includes many independent agencies. These agencies collect information that can help with lawmaking. An agency can include thousands of individuals. Congress creates independent agencies. It passes a statute that grants each agency the authority to oversee a specific industry or area. The statute provides clear guidelines and goals. It also defines the agency's authority to enact rules and regulations.

A board of approximately five to seven individuals heads each agency. The president selects the board members. The Senate then confirms the nominees. Board members serve for four-year terms. The terms are staggered so that an entire board does not need to be replaced at once. Board members may not have regular communication with the president. Though the president is allowed to dismiss cabinet members at anytime, he or she must have a reason to dismiss a board member. Board members can be removed for reasons such as neglect of duty.

Carol M. Browner was appointed as administrator of the Environmental Protection Agency (EPA) in 1993 and remained in that post until 2001. When she left, Browner was the longest-serving EPA administrator in history.

The SEC is an independent agency that helps regulate the economy. It protects investors by overseeing the country's securities markets. The Environmental Protection Agency (EPA) was established in the 1970s. It works to reduce air pollution, regulate pesticide use, and help state and local governments address environmental issues. Another well-known independent agency is the National Aeronautics and Space Administration (NASA). NASA is the US space program. It includes approximately 18,000 employees who research space and space travel.

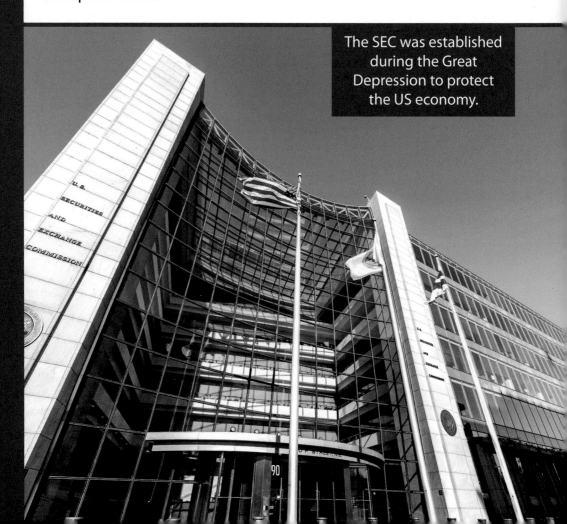

The SEC was established during the Great Depression to protect the US economy.

NASA is responsible for developing spacecraft and space technology that will improve the future of space travel.

The US Postal Service delivers mail worldwide and handles 46 percent of the world's mail.

GOVERNMENT CORPORATIONS

Government corporations are parts of the executive branch. They provide valuable services to citizens. Unlike cabinet departments and independent agencies, government corporations charge fees for their services and compete with private companies.

The US Postal Service (USPS) is one of the best-known government corporations. It provides mail and delivery services to

The National Park Service protects landscapes and wildlife. The National Park Foundation is a related government corporation that collects donations to improve national parks.

people and businesses in the United States and around the world. It charges for these services. USPS competes against private companies such as FedEx and the United Parcel Service (UPS). Another government corporation is the Tennessee

Amtrak includes 21,000 miles (33,796 km) of railroads in 46 states as well as Washington, DC, and parts of Canada.

Valley Authority. It provides low-cost electricity, flood control, navigation, and land management in the southeastern United States. Amtrak is a government corporation too. It provides rail transportation for people and goods.

LEGISLATIVE BRANCH

The US Capitol stands 288 feet (88 m) tall at its highest point.

The legislative branch is the only branch of government with the power to pass laws. Congress is the main legislative body. It includes the House of Representatives and the Senate. Members of Congress meet and work in the US Capitol building in Washington, DC.

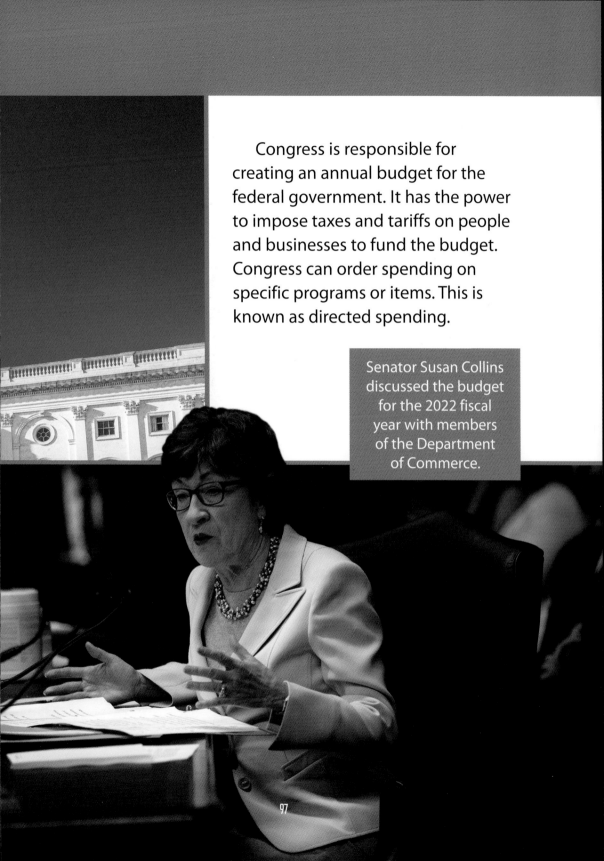

Congress is responsible for creating an annual budget for the federal government. It has the power to impose taxes and tariffs on people and businesses to fund the budget. Congress can order spending on specific programs or items. This is known as directed spending.

Senator Susan Collins discussed the budget for the 2022 fiscal year with members of the Department of Commerce.

Congress also has investigative powers. Members of both houses spend time attending hearings. They conduct investigations in committees. Congress can issue a subpoena. This is an official request that forces a person to turn over evidence. A subpoena can also force someone to speak about a particular issue. A person can be charged with a crime if he or she refuses to respond to a subpoena.

The legislative branch has the power to declare war. Congress made its first declaration of war in 1812. Since then, Congress has declared war ten additional times. Most recently, Congress declared war against several countries in 1941 and 1942 during World War II (1939–1945). Congress has also passed

Congress declared war on Japan following the attack on Pearl Harbor in Hawaii in 1941.

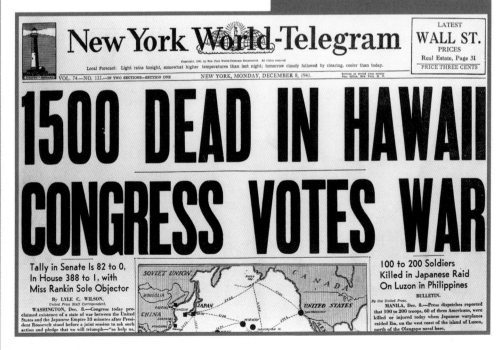

Members of Congress hosted a ceremony in September 2021, marking the twentieth anniversary of the September 11 terrorist attacks.

resolutions to allow military force. For example, terrorists attacked the United States on September 11, 2001. Congress passed a joint resolution to allow the use of military force against those responsible.

The legislative branch includes independent agencies. These agencies help Congress create new laws. They check other branches of government. The Government Accountability Office (GAO) is an independent legislative agency. It reviews how the government is spending taxpayer money. It makes sure the money is used to improve the country. The GAO performs an annual review of government spending. It suggests ways to correct errors if it finds that funds were

The Government Accountability Office celebrated its 100-year anniversary in 2021.

United States Government Accountability Office

441 G Street, NW

In 2021, representatives Young Kim, *left*, and Michelle Park Steel, *right*, along with Marilyn Strickland, became the first Korean American women in Congress.

handled improperly. These are called corrective actions. The GAO figures out the root cause of the spending error. It takes steps to make sure the errors do not occur again.

THE HOUSE OF REPRESENTATIVES

The House of Representatives consists of 435 elected members from the 50 states. A state's population is proportional to the number of representatives it has. States with larger populations have more representatives than states with smaller populations. There are also six nonvoting members in the House of Representatives. They represent the District of Columbia and five US territories. These territories are Puerto Rico, American Samoa, Guam, the US Virgin Islands, and the Northern Mariana Islands.

Sam Rayburn was the longest-serving Speaker of the House, with 17 years in the position.

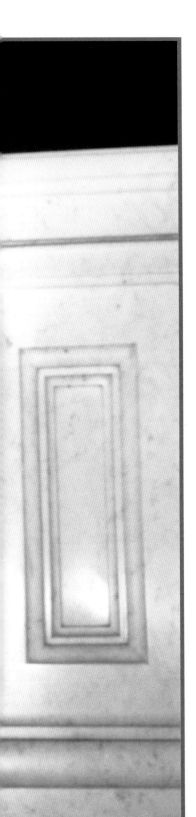

The Speaker of the House is the leader of the House of Representatives. The Speaker oversees debates. He or she also appoints committee members and performs other duties. The majority and minority political parties of the House submit candidates to be the Speaker of the House. The representatives vote for a candidate from this list. A Speaker of the House is elected every two years.

A person must be at least 25 years old to be a representative. He or she must be a US citizen for a minimum of seven years. The person must be a resident of the state he or she represents. Representatives serve a two-year term. There are no term limits for representatives.

The House of Representatives has several powers and responsibilities. The House can initiate a revenue bill. This is a bill that raises money through taxes and tariffs. The House may also get involved in presidential elections. The Electoral College is the body of people that elect the president. The House elects the president if there is a tie in the Electoral College. The House also has the power to impeach federal officials, including the president.

Representatives serve on various committees. There are approximately 20 permanent committees. They focus on different policy areas such as the budget and foreign affairs. Other committees are formed temporarily to handle specific projects. Each committee oversees agencies, programs, and activities that fall within its area of focus. Committees are led by majority party members. They hold hearings, propose bills for review, and conduct investigations. Some bills do not make it out of committee. Others are passed on to the full House for further discussion and voting.

IMPEACHMENT

The practice of impeachment began in England. It was also used in the colonies. The Founding Fathers gave the legislative branch the impeachment power. This would prevent a government branch from abusing its powers. Congress can charge and try a federal official for "treason, bribery, or other high crimes and misdemeanors" during the impeachment process. The Constitution does not define "high crimes and misdemeanors." People often debate what actions qualify for impeachment.

THE SENATE

The Senate is made up of 100 senators. Each state has two senators. State legislatures chose a state's senators until 1913. This changed when the Seventeenth Amendment was passed. It stated that senators would be elected by popular vote of a state's citizens.

Senator Chuck Grassley is one of the longest-serving senators in US history, with more than 40 years in Congress.

A person must be at least 30 years old to run for the Senate. He or she must be a US citizen for a minimum of nine years and must also be a resident of the state he or she represents. Senators serve six-year terms. Their terms are staggered so that approximately one-third of senators reach the end of their terms every two years. There is no term limit for senators.

Charles Schumer, *left*, and Mitch McConnell, *right*, both served as Senate leaders.

Senators elect floor leaders every two years. These are the Senate majority leader and the Senate minority leader. They represent different political parties. Members of the party elect their leader. The party with more members in the Senate elects the majority leader. For example, Democrats outnumbered Republicans in the Senate in 2021. Democrats selected

Charles E. Schumer to be the Senate majority leader. Republicans chose Mitch McConnell as the Senate minority leader.

The Senate is responsible for confirming nominees to federal positions. The president has the power to nominate federal judges and cabinet members. These appointments must be confirmed by a majority vote in the Senate. The Senate rarely rejects nominees. But it is more likely to reject a nominee when most Senate members belong to a different political party

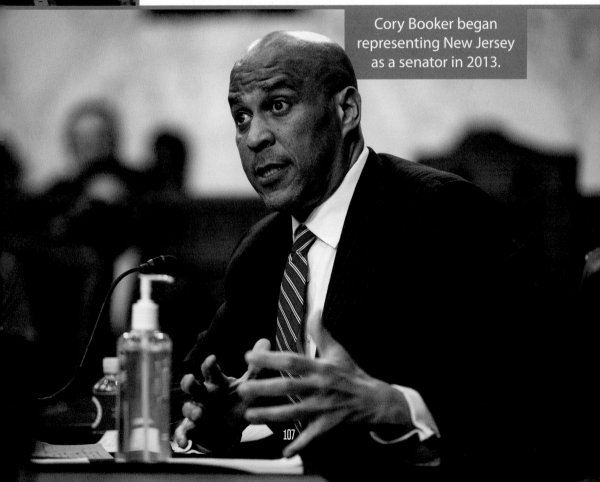

Cory Booker began representing New Jersey as a senator in 2013.

than the president. The Senate may also reject a nomination if the candidate is not qualified for the position. Some members have voted against the confirmation of federal judges. They believed the nominee's political beliefs would interfere with fair rulings. The Constitution also grants the Senate the power to ratify treaties. Treaties that involve foreign trade must also be approved by the House.

The Senate has a role in the impeachment process. The House of Representatives sends articles of impeachment to the Senate. The Senate holds a trial to review and consider

In 1868, Andrew Johnson became the first US president to be impeached. US senators then voted on whether to convict or acquit him.

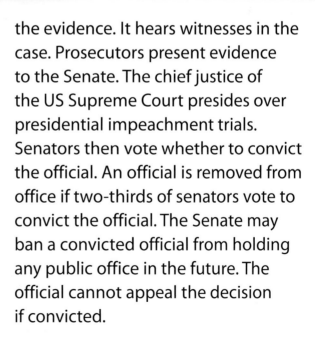

The Senate convicted former federal judge G. Thomas Porteous Jr., *center*, for accepting bribes in 2010. Porteous was removed from office and banned from holding future office.

the evidence. It hears witnesses in the case. Prosecutors present evidence to the Senate. The chief justice of the US Supreme Court presides over presidential impeachment trials. Senators then vote whether to convict the official. An official is removed from office if two-thirds of senators vote to convict the official. The Senate may ban a convicted official from holding any public office in the future. The official cannot appeal the decision if convicted.

Senator Jon Tester, *right*, of the Senate Appropriations Committee talks to members of the Department of Defense after discussing the department's 2023 budget.

Andrew Johnson, Bill Clinton, and Donald Trump are the only US presidents to be impeached. Trump was impeached twice. None of the presidents were convicted. Trump's second impeachment was the twenty-first impeachment in US history. Eight federal officials have been found guilty and banned from running for future office. Three officials resigned before they could be charged.

CENSURE AND EXPULSION

Under the Constitution, the Senate can determine the rules for punishing or expelling a senator. Senate members can censure other senators for inappropriate conduct. A censure is a formal statement of disapproval. It takes the form of a resolution and receives a majority vote. A censure does not remove a senator from office. But it can damage a senator's reputation. The Senate can expel a member for serious offenses. Fifteen senators have been expelled. Fourteen of these senators were expelled during the Civil War for supporting the Confederacy.

The Senate has committees. Senate committees gather information through hearings and investigations. They draft, debate, and recommend bills to the full Senate. Only a few bills considered in the Senate's committees are presented to the full Senate.

Both the House and the Senate have committees that focus on government oversight. For example, the Senate Committee on Homeland Security and Government Affairs analyzes federal agencies and departments. The committee makes sure these organizations are working efficiently and effectively.

MAKING LAWS

There are several steps in the legislative process. They involve both houses of Congress. The first step is the introduction of a bill to Congress. Any person can write a bill. But only representatives or senators can introduce a bill to Congress. Bills can be presented in either the House or the Senate. The initial draft of a bill may go through many changes throughout the legislative process.

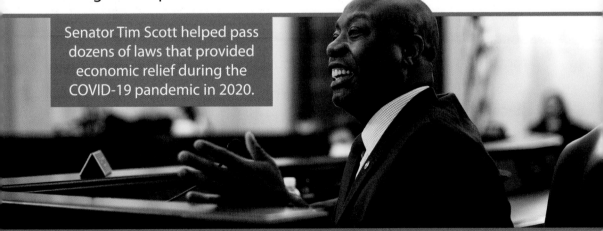

Senator Tim Scott helped pass dozens of laws that provided economic relief during the COVID-19 pandemic in 2020.

People can call their senators and representatives to show support for legislation.

The appropriate committee reviews the bill. There are many committees in both the House and Senate. Each committee specializes in a particular policy area. Some committees are made of subcommittees that focus on a more specific policy area. A subcommittee reviews and considers a bill. It may decide to accept, amend, or reject the bill. After it accepted by the subcommittee, the bill moves to the full committee. The full committee reviews the bill again. Subcommittees and committees may hold hearings to review a bill. They may invite experts, advocates, and critics to discuss the bill.

The bill moves to the floor of the House or Senate after being approved by the full committee. The Speaker of the House may place the bill on the House's calendar for consideration. The Senate majority leader can make a motion to proceed with the bill. Some bills are considered by the full House or Senate immediately. Others may not be considered for months. Some are never scheduled for consideration.

Paul Ryan, *front left*, signed the Tax Cuts and Jobs Act in 2017. The bill aimed to reduce taxes for individuals and businesses.

Debate on a bill follows a structured process in the House. Any representative may speak about the bill. But representatives can speak only for a few minutes. They are also limited in the number and type of amendment they can propose. Representatives vote on the bill after the debate has ended. A simple majority approves the bill. Then the bill is

PROTECT OUR EARTH

THE WORLD WATCHIN

ONES WE V
ITING FOR

Organized protests are one way people can draw attention to important issues that lawmakers can address.

sent to the Senate. If the Senate is the first to review and approve a bill, the bill is sent to the House for its approval. A bill must be passed by both houses before it is sent to the president. The bill dies if either house does not pass the bill. Representatives may choose to amend the bill before moving forward with the vote.

Senators can make any number or type of amendments to a proposed bill. They also have an unlimited amount of time to debate a bill. They may talk about the bill or discuss other topics. This method of continuing a debate to delay a vote is called a filibuster. It is a way to protect the minority opinion.

Federal workers protested after the US government shut down in 2019 because of a Democratic filibuster.

I AM A FEDERAL EMPLOYEE.

I AM A FEDERAL EMPLOYEE.

my 20th day
g locked out
f my job.

NTEU.org

This is my 20th day of being locked out of my job.

NTEU National Treasury

NTEU.org

We're
ED

Senator Steve Daines spoke to reporters after a cloture vote in 2018 that resulted in confirming Brett Kavanaugh to the Supreme Court.

But people became frustrated with the filibuster in the late 1800s because it slowed down governmental procedures. The Senate passed a rule for cloture in 1917. Cloture is a procedure to end a filibuster. Senators could end a filibuster with a two-thirds vote. The number of votes needed for cloture was lowered to a sixty-percent vote in 1975. A vote on the bill follows a cloture. A bill passes through the Senate with a simple majority.

President George H. W. Bush signed the Americans with Disabilities Act into law in 1990 after it was passed by Congress.

Under the Constitution, the bills passed by the House and Senate must have identical wording. Bills may undergo many changes while they are passed by the individual houses. A Conference Committee made up of members of the House and Senate meets to create a final identical version of the bill. They write a conference report. Then the House and Senate each vote to pass the conference report. Congress sends the bill to the president after the report is passed by both houses.

The president has several options after a bill arrives from Congress. The president can sign the bill into law. He or she may also veto a bill. Congress has the power to override a presidential veto with a two-thirds vote of the House and Senate. The bill becomes law if the override is successful. The president may choose not to veto the bill or sign it into law. The bill automatically becomes law if the president does not act on it within ten days and Congress is in session. If Congress is not in session and the president does not act within ten days, the bill dies. This is called a pocket veto. Congress cannot override a pocket veto. Congress must start the legislative process again if it wants to pass the bill.

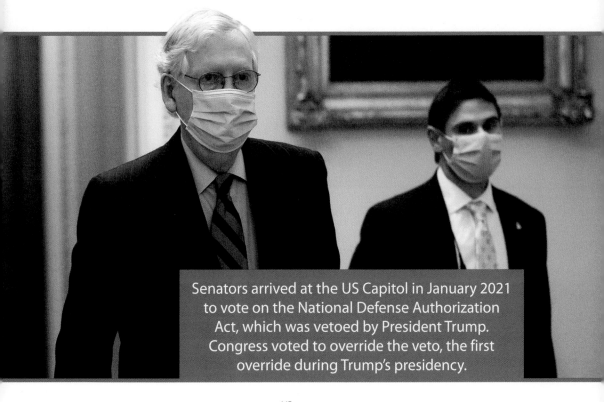

Senators arrived at the US Capitol in January 2021 to vote on the National Defense Authorization Act, which was vetoed by President Trump. Congress voted to override the veto, the first override during Trump's presidency.

JUDICIAL BRANCH

Though the judicial branch was established at the country's founding, the Supreme Court did not have its own building until 1935.

The judicial branch is responsible for interpreting laws. It determines how to apply laws to real-life cases. The judicial branch also reviews federal laws and decides if they follow the Constitution.

The judicial branch checks and balances the powers of the other branches. It can remove laws passed by Congress if

they are unconstitutional. It can also remove presidential acts. For example, the Biden administration attempted to enforce a vaccine mandate in 2022. It would have required employees in large businesses to be vaccinated against COVID-19 or show a negative COVID-19 test. The Supreme Court blocked this mandate. It said the executive branch did not have the power to make major decisions about public health.

JUDICIARY ACT OF 1789

The Judiciary Act of 1789 created the three-part federal court system. The act created a judiciary that is composed of district courts, courts of appeals, and the US Supreme Court. The act divides the United States into districts. Each district has a court and a judge. It has lawyers responsible for civil and criminal cases too. The act also created the Office of the Attorney General to serve as the head of the Department of Justice.

Activists stood outside the Supreme Court in support of its decision to protect Deferred Action for Childhood Arrivals (DACA) in June 2020.

The Supreme Court is the highest court in the land. The Supreme Court and other federal courts such as courts of appeals and district courts make up the judicial branch.

Together these courts make sure US laws are applied properly. They work to ensure people who have broken the law are sentenced fairly.

Supporters of Ketanji Brown Jackson gathered in Washington, DC, as senators decided whether to confirm her nomination to the Supreme Court.

THE SUPREME COURT

The Supreme Court is the only part of the judicial branch that the Constitution specifically requires. It does not describe a set number of justices. Congress decides the size of the Supreme Court. The number of justices has ranged from five to ten. The Supreme Court has included eight associate justices and a chief justice since 1869. The chief justice is the leader of the Supreme Court. He or she has more influence than the other justices when deciding which cases the Supreme Court should hear. The chief justice also leads discussions about the cases. The opinion of the chief justice is equal to the opinions of the associate justices.

There have been discussions to adjust the number of justices. In 2021, Democrats in Congress introduced a bill that would expand the Supreme Court to 13 justices. But many people, including President Joe Biden, disagreed. Expanding the Supreme Court would allow the sitting president to appoint new justices that aligned with his or her political beliefs. Former justice Ruth Bader Ginsburg also thought this would cause the Supreme Court to become increasingly partisan.

Clarence Thomas was sworn in as an associate justice in October 1991, becoming the second Black justice in US history.

Ketanji Brown Jackson was born on September 14, 1970, in Washington, DC. Her family moved to Miami, Florida, when she was young, and Jackson attended high school there. She went to college at Harvard University in Cambridge, Massachusetts. Jackson continued her education at Harvard Law School.

Her education gave her the skills she needed to become a lawyer. She was a law clerk for Justice Stephen Breyer from 1999 to 2000. Jackson also worked in private law firms and for

Jackson became the sixth female justice in US history.

the US Sentencing Commission. Jackson served as an assistant federal public defender from 2005 to 2007. Public defenders provide legal defense for people who cannot afford a lawyer.

Jackson became a federal judge in 2013. She was nominated to the US District Court in Washington, DC, by President Barack Obama and confirmed by the Senate. Biden promoted her to the US Court of Appeals in 2021. Breyer announced his retirement from the Supreme Court in January 2022. Biden nominated Jackson to fill his position. The Senate confirmed the nomination on April 7, 2022, making Jackson the first Black female justice in US history.

Jackson stands besides Stephen Breyer, the Supreme Court justice that she replaced.

Sandra Day O'Connor made history when she was confirmed by the Senate to replace Potter Stewart on the Supreme Court in 1981. O'Connor was the first female justice.

When there is a vacancy on the Court, the president nominates a new justice. The Constitution does not list qualifications for justices. A justice does not need to be a lawyer or law school graduate. But all justices in US history have had some legal training. Justice James F. Byrnes served on the Court in 1941 and 1942. Byrnes did not graduate from high school. He taught himself law before passing the bar exam.

The Senate must approve the president's nominee to the Supreme Court. Once approved, the new justice is sworn in. Justices hold their positions for life. They can be more impartial when deciding cases because they do not run for office. Justices do not face the same political pressure as elected officials. They do not worry if their decisions are popular. Justices can focus on applying the law without outside influence. This idea is called judicial independence.

Jackson and Biden watch as the Senate votes to confirm Jackson to the Supreme Court.

Thurgood Marshall became the Court's first Black justice in 1967.

Most of the cases the Supreme Court hears are appeals cases. This means they are reviewing the decisions made by lower courts. The Supreme Court does not typically hold a formal trial. It looks at the laws involved in the case. Then it provides judgement on whether the law was applied justly.

The Supreme Court does not hear every appeal. Approximately 7,000 cases are appealed to the Supreme Court each year. The Supreme Court agrees to hear fewer than 150 of those cases. It typically hears cases that involve different interpretations of the same law. For example, two federal courts of appeals may have made different rulings on cases that involve the same law. The Supreme Court may decide to hear the case. It will determine how the law should be applied. The Court also often choses to hear cases that involve the interpretation of the Constitution.

Abortion rights and pro-life activists both rallied in front of the Supreme Court building as justices reviewed a case about abortion laws in June 2022.

The parties involved must petition the Court to hear the case. If four of the justices decide the Court should review the case, the Court grants a writ of certiorari. This is the formal request to receive the case information from a lower court. The parties involved must also submit legal briefs to the justices. The parties will appear before the Court for oral arguments. They present their case and answer questions from the justices. *Amicus curiae*, or "friends of the court," may submit legal briefs for the case with permission from the Supreme Court. Amicus curiae includes industry trade groups, academic experts, and the US government. They may provide guidance about a ruling.

At 48 years old, Amy Coney Barrett was the youngest female justice in US history when she was appointed.

John Roberts was sworn
in as chief justice in
September 2005.

The justices meet privately to discuss the case after oral
arguments. It usually takes several months before the Supreme
Court issues its decision. When the Court releases its official
decision, justices who support the decision may write a
concurring opinion. Those who disagree may write a dissenting
opinion explaining their perspective.

The decision of the Supreme Court is final. The ruling cannot be appealed. Supreme Court decisions set a precedent that lower courts must follow. But the Court can overturn a previous Supreme Court ruling. For example, the 1896 Supreme Court case *Plessy v. Ferguson* ruled that segregation was constitutional. The Supreme Court overturned this decision in 1954 in the *Brown v. Board of Education* case.

School integration following the *Brown v. Board of Education* ruling was a slow process. Protesters marched for equal rights and integrated schools in 1963.

Federal courts of appeals, including the DC Court of Appeals, hear approximately 50,000 cases each year.

In some instances, the Supreme Court is the first and only court to hear a case. This includes cases in which there is conflict between two states. The Supreme Court also oversees trials that involve high-ranking federal officials.

THE FEDERAL COURTS

The US Supreme Court is the only court required explicitly by the Constitution. But the Constitution also gives Congress the power to establish lower federal courts. Congress has used this power to create a system of US district courts. These courts are often the first to hear cases that involve federal laws. Every state has at least one federal district court. There are also 13 courts of appeal that hear appeal cases that were initially tried in federal district courts. If the parties continue to appeal, the case may eventually be heard at the Supreme Court.

Sonia Sotomayor was a judge in the federal courts before being nominated as the first Latina justice on the Supreme Court in May 2009.

Like Supreme Court justices, judges in federal courts are appointed by the president and confirmed by the Senate. Federal judges do not have a fixed term. They serve until they retire or die. They can be removed if impeached by the House and convicted by the Senate.

Federal courts interpret the law, determine if the law is constitutional, and apply their decision to an individual case. Federal courts can subpoena parties to force them to turn over evidence and testify. Federal courts follow the decisions of the Supreme Court. They apply the Supreme Court's interpretation of a law to any future cases they may hear.

US COURT OF FEDERAL CLAIMS

Congress established the US Court of Federal Claims in 1982. This court handles cases that involve the United States or any of its branches, agencies, or departments as a defendant. The court also handles cases that involve federal laws, executive regulations, contracts with the government, and money claims against the United States.

William Rehnquist, *left*, served as chief justice of the Supreme Court from 1986 to 2005. He was one of 402 federal judges appointed by Reagan, the most judicial appointments of any US president.

CRIMINAL AND CIVIL CASES

There are two types of legal cases in the United States: criminal cases and civil cases. Criminal cases involve crimes and actions deemed to be harmful to society. These include cases about murder, assault, drug offenses, and more. Civil cases include divorce proceedings, personal injury cases, contract disputes, employee discrimination trials, and other cases.

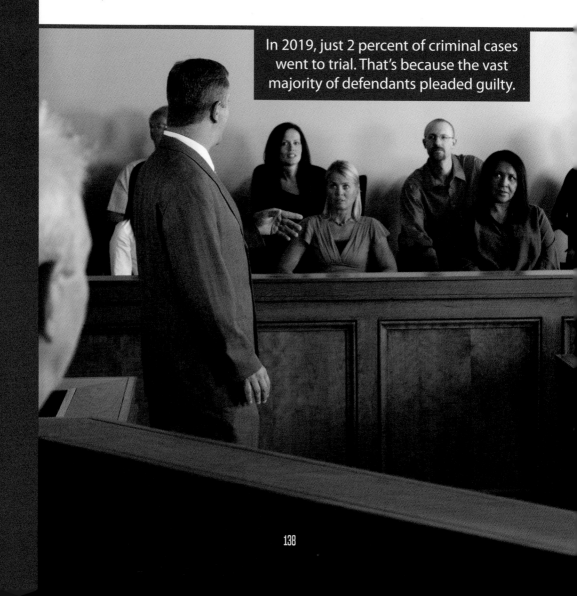

In 2019, just 2 percent of criminal cases went to trial. That's because the vast majority of defendants pleaded guilty.

The judicial process for criminal cases usually begins when law enforcement arrests a person for a crime. The accused person is tried in either a state or federal court, depending on the law broken and the type of crime. The accused will appear in court before a judge and be formally charged with a crime. The person enters a plea of guilty or not guilty.

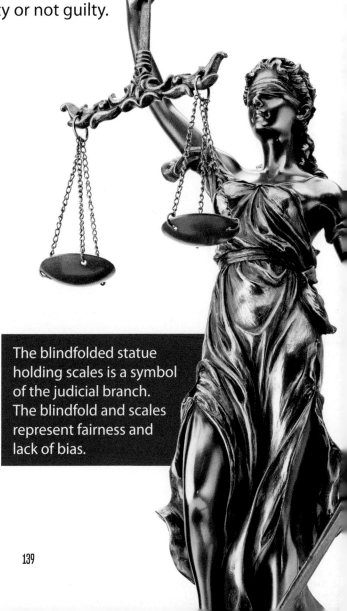

The blindfolded statue holding scales is a symbol of the judicial branch. The blindfold and scales represent fairness and lack of bias.

Judges are responsible for fairly sentencing defendants who are found guilty.

Federal crimes are prosecuted through the US attorney's office in a federal court. The state attorney's office prosecutes crimes in state court. The defendant and his or her legal team have time to review the evidence in the case before the trial. They use this time to craft a legal argument. A judge presides over the trial and courtroom. The prosecution and the defense present their sides. They offer evidence and witness testimony to support their legal arguments. A jury decides the case. Criminal charges are dismissed if the jury finds a defendant not guilty. The judge decides the defendant's sentence if the jury returns a guilty verdict. Sentences can include fines, prison time, or even the death penalty.

A civil case begins when one party, called the plaintiff, files a lawsuit against the defendant. The parties meet in a civil court to resolve the dispute. For example, a plaintiff may sue a defendant for not fulfilling the terms of a legal contract.

Judges may allow people to participate in community service, such as training service dogs, to reduce their sentences.

FREE SPEECH
4
STUDENTS

Many civil cases are heard in state courts. Plaintiffs may also file a civil lawsuit in federal court if they claim constitutional rights or federal statutes have been violated. *Tinker v. Des Moines Independent Community School District* was a federal civil case that looked at the First Amendment. In December 1965, some students in Des Moines, Iowa, wore black armbands

E SPEECH
4
UDENTS

FREE SPEECH
4
STUDENTS

Several civil cases about freedom of speech in schools have made their way to the Supreme Court.

to protest the Vietnam War (1954–1975). The school sent these students home. The parents of these students sued the school district for violating freedom of speech. But the federal courts ruled that schools have the right to discipline their students and prevent behaviors that may interfere with learning.

Both the defense and prosecution are allowed to call on and question a witness.

Lawyers for both the plaintiff and defendant gather evidence in civil cases. They may call upon witnesses to testify. In some cases, a jury decides whether the accused person is guilty. Parties can also agree to waive their right to a jury trial and have the case decided by a judge. If the case is decided in favor of the plaintiff, the judge may award the plaintiff monetary damages. The judge may also order the defendant to fulfill a legal duty or stop illegal activity.

THE US SENTENCING COMMISSION

The US Sentencing Commission is an independent agency of the judicial branch. It was created in 1984 to make sure federal courts were consistent with their sentencing. The Sentencing Commission provides guidelines to the courts. This helps ensure similar crimes are judged similarly. The commission also works with the legislative and executive branches. Together, they create policies that can help prevent crimes in the future.

The Thurgood Marshall Federal Judiciary Building houses several judicial agencies, including the US Sentencing Commission.

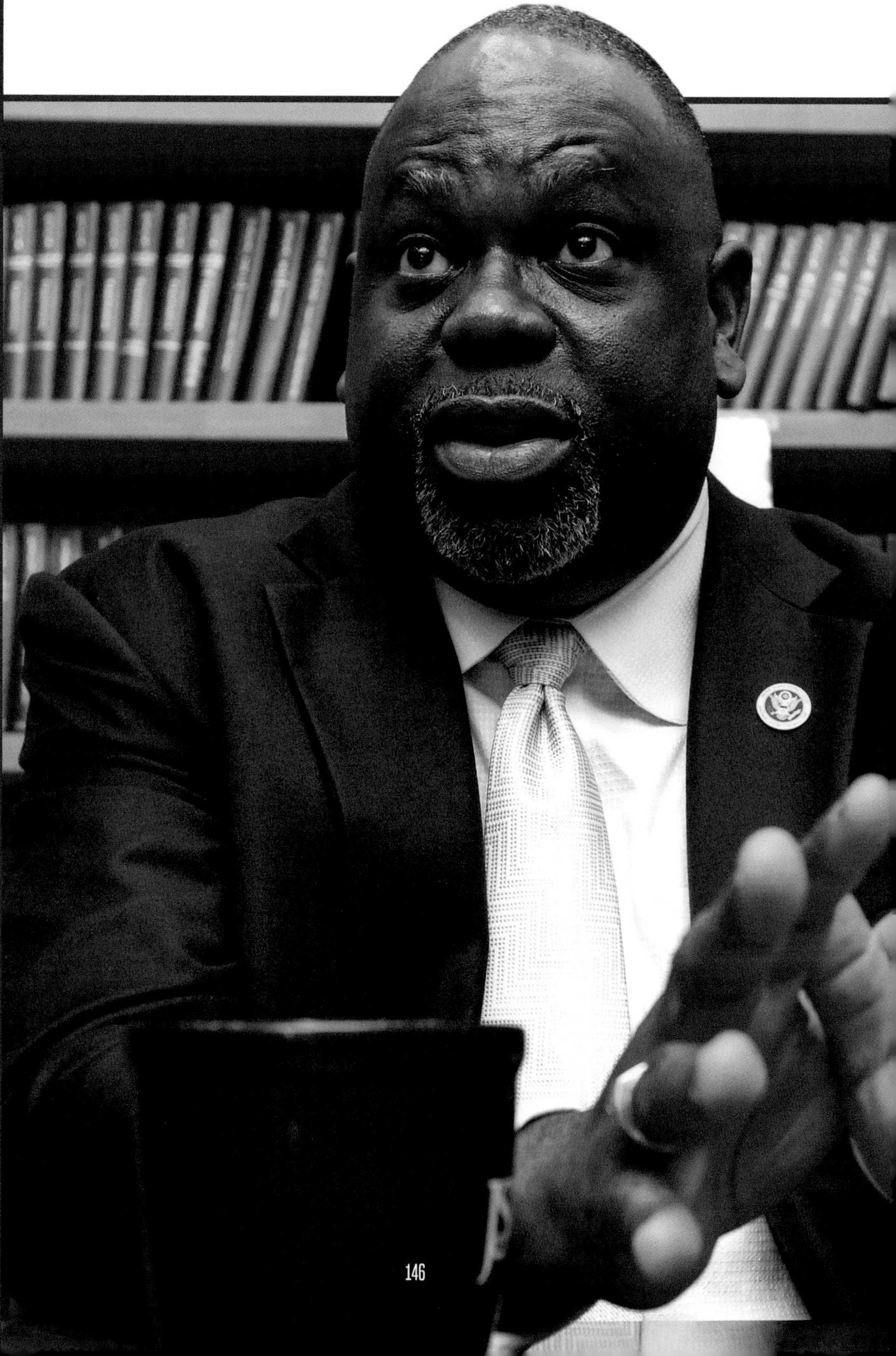

The Sentencing Commission is led by seven members. These members are nominated by the president and confirmed by the Senate. Each member serves a six-year term. The terms are staggered so that the entire board does not need to be replaced at once. In addition, the Sentencing Commission oversees five offices and hundreds of employees. These offices suggest sentencing guidelines and assess the work of judges.

The Senate confirmed Carlton Reeves to be a member of the US Sentencing Commission in August 2022.

VOTING

Voting is one way people can have a say in how the government is run.

One of the most important rights in the United States is voting. Today, citizens who are at least 18 are eligible to vote in local, state, and federal elections. The right to vote is protected in the US Constitution. It cannot be denied based on

a person's gender, race, religion, disability, or sexual orientation. In most states, citizens must have lived in the state for a certain amount of time in order to vote. They must also be registered to vote.

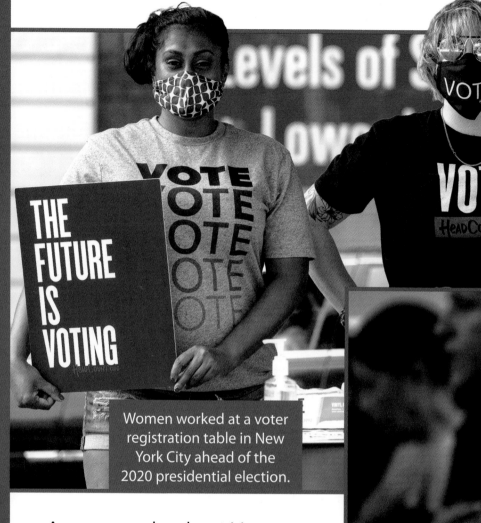

Women worked at a voter registration table in New York City ahead of the 2020 presidential election.

A person needs to be a citizen to vote in US elections. Noncitizens, including permanent legal residents, are not eligible to vote in federal and state elections. Most local elections also bar noncitizens. A few allow permanent legal residents to vote. People with felony convictions or

severe mental disabilities do not have the right to vote in some states. People born in US territories are considered US citizens. But they are not allowed to vote in federal elections while living in the territory.

Immigrants go through the naturalization process to become citizens. After being naturalized, they are able to vote.

THE HISTORY OF VOTING RIGHTS

Voting rights were not granted to every citizen at the country's founding. The Constitution initially allowed states to decide who could vote. States limited voting rights to white male property owners for many decades. Some states used religious tests to make sure only Christian men were voting.

People continue to fight for equal voting rights today.

Over time, these voting restrictions began to loosen. In the early 1800s, many states began to remove property requirements for voting. The Fifteenth Amendment was ratified in 1870. This amendment prohibited states from denying a person the right to vote based on race. But several states implemented other barriers to stop Black men from voting. Many states used poll taxes. They required a tax payment to

In August 2021, thousands of people participated in the March On for Voting Rights protest to support legislation that would make voting easily accessible.

★★ I SUPPORT H.R. 4 ★★★

✓ THE JOHN R. LEWIS VOTING RIGHTS ADVANCEMENT ACT

★★★ I SU

✓ THE VOTIN ADVAN

register to vote. This was meant to make it more difficult for Black Americans and poor white people to vote. Some states also required literacy tests. Many Black men had been formerly enslaved. They did not have easy access to education or money. This made it hard to pass literacy tests and pay poll taxes. Voting was still limited to only men at this time.

RT H.R. 4 ★★★

The women's suffrage movement was growing in the late 1800s. Women held state campaigns, marches, and protests. They petitioned Congress for the right to vote. Wyoming became the first state to grant women this right in 1890. By 1915, women had voting rights in 15 states. The Nineteenth Amendment was ratified in 1920. It gave women the right to vote across the country.

Many suffragists participated in peaceful marches and parades in the late 1800s and early 1900s.

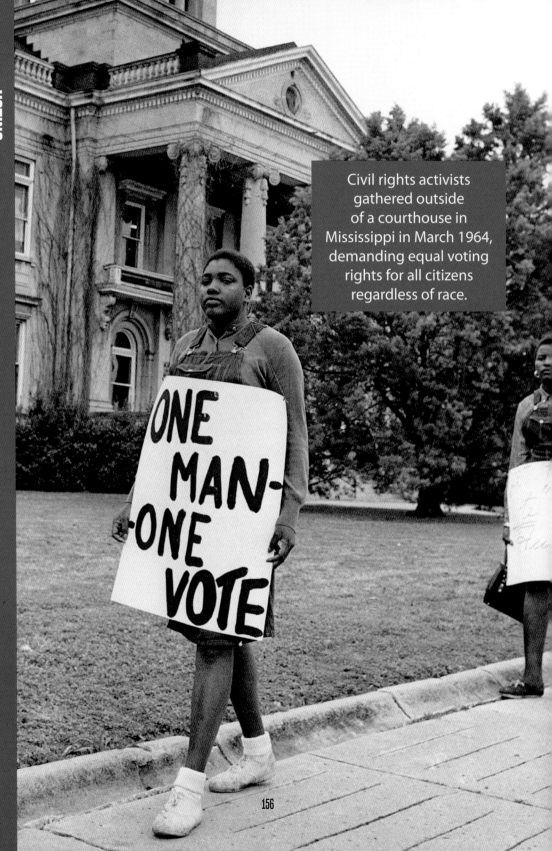

VOTING

ONE
MAN-
-ONE
VOTE

Civil rights activists
gathered outside
of a courthouse in
Mississippi in March 1964,
demanding equal voting
rights for all citizens
regardless of race.

Many states continued to add barriers to voting. They made voting more difficult for people of color, immigrants, and low-income citizens through the mid-1900s. These barriers included literacy tests, poll taxes, and other restrictions. Black people also sometimes faced violence if they tried to register to vote. Many were afraid to register or vote in elections. As a result, they were not well-represented in government. Many women of color faced similar barriers even after the Nineteenth Amendment was passed.

Rosa Parks, *right*, protested segregation when she refused to give up her bus seat for a white man.

The Civil Rights Movement gained ground in the 1950s and 1960s. Black Americans led protests against racial discrimination. They advocated for equal rights. They made their

voices heard through peaceful protests. These actions included boycotts, marches, and sit-ins. For example, civil rights activists set up a bus boycott in 1955 to protest segregated seating on buses.

In 1961, a group of Black and white activists known as Freedom Riders rode on buses through southern states. Many of the bus stations were still segregated despite a federal ban on segregation.

Martin Luther King Jr. led a march from Selma to Montgomery in March 1965. Thousands of people participated.

The Twenty-Fourth Amendment was ratified in 1964. It banned the use of poll taxes in national elections. But poll taxes could still be used in state and local elections. There was still much work to be done. In 1964 and 1965, civil rights leaders organized several peaceful demonstrations to protest the lack of equal voting rights for Black Americans. They led a march in Selma, Alabama, to support efforts to register Black voters in the city. State troopers and police attacked the marchers. The march drew national attention. It helped shine a spotlight on the issue of voting rights. It also convinced President Lyndon B. Johnson and Congress to pass important voting rights legislation in 1965.

THE VOTING RIGHTS ACT OF 1965

On August 6, 1965, President Johnson signed the Voting Rights Act into law. The Act prohibited discriminatory voting practices and requirements. It banned denying a citizen the right to vote based on race. It also outlawed literacy tests for voting. In addition, the act established the appointment of federal examiners who had the power to register citizens to vote.

Civil rights activists demonstrated the need for the Voting Rights Act, which President Lyndon B. Johnson signed into law after it passed through Congress.

161

The Voting Rights Act also expanded on the Twenty-Fourth Amendment. It challenged the use of poll taxes in state and local elections. This issue was brought to the Supreme Court. In 1966, the Court decided any use of a poll tax in any election was unconstitutional.

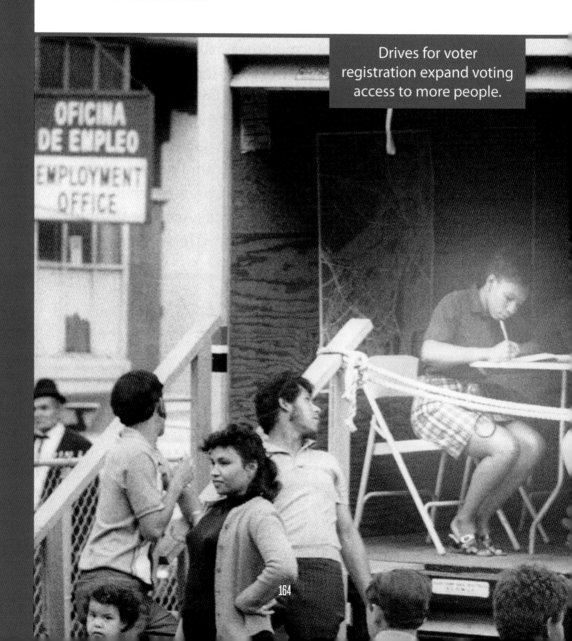

Drives for voter registration expand voting access to more people.

The Voting Rights Act added federal oversight of states and local jurisdictions. This oversight focused on places with a history of suppressing voter rights based on race. The act required these places to get federal approval if they wanted to change their election laws. The Voting Rights Act was very

effective in discouraging new barriers to voting in the following decades. It also gave communities and civil rights activists a way to stay informed about proposals that could affect voting rights.

Because of the Voting Rights Act, thousands of new Black voters were able to participate in elections.

In *South Carolina v. Katzenbach*, the state filed a complaint against US Attorney General Nicholas Katzenbach, *center*, about the Voting Rights Act. The Supreme Court ruled 8–1 in favor of Katzenbach.

The Voting Rights Act had a significant impact on the relationship between the federal and state governments. Several states challenged the act in the courts. In the 1966 case *South Carolina v. Katzenbach*, South Carolina claimed that the act violated the state's right to run its own elections. It claimed that federal examiners should not be able to investigate the state's election practices. The Supreme Court dismissed the challenge. It ruled that Congress had the power to prevent racial discrimination in voting. The Supreme Court made several important rulings that upheld the legislation in the 1960s. The passage of the Voting Rights Act immediately improved access to voting for people of color. By the end of 1965, approximately 250,000 Black Americans had registered to vote for the first time.

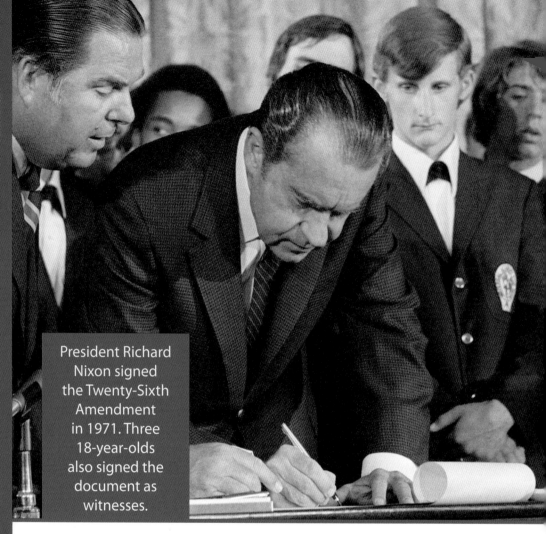

President Richard Nixon signed the Twenty-Sixth Amendment in 1971. Three 18-year-olds also signed the document as witnesses.

EXPANDING VOTING RIGHTS

The Constitution originally limited voting to people who were 21 or older. A movement to lower the voting age gained popularity in the 1960s. The United States was engaged in the Vietnam War. Soldiers who were 18 years old were sent overseas to fight in the war. People argued that if 18-year-olds could serve in war, they should also be old enough to vote. The Twenty-Sixth Amendment was ratified in 1971. It lowered the voting age to 18.

Congress expanded the Voting Rights Act to include protections for citizens who spoke languages other than English in 1975. Places with large numbers of voters who do not speak English had to provide voting materials in other languages. They also had to have language assistance at the polls on Election Day. In 1982, Congress added a provision to the act. It required states to make voting more accessible for older voters and those with disabilities.

Polling places are required to help voters with disabilities if they need assistance.

ctVRA

PROTECT
MY
VOTE

Hundreds of people protested outside the Supreme Court building during the *Shelby County v. Holder* case.

CHALLENGES FOR VOTING RIGHTS

In June 2013, the Supreme Court struck down part of the Voting Rights Act. The Supreme Court reached a decision in the *Shelby County v. Holder* case. It said states and local jurisdictions no longer had to submit election changes to the federal government for approval. The Supreme Court decided that this part of the Voting Rights Act was unconstitutional. It reasoned that the requirement made sense when the Voting Rights Act was first passed.

NATIONAL VOTER REGISTRATION ACT

Congress passed the National Voter Registration Act (NVRA) to increase voter registration rates in 1993. NVRA requires states to allow citizens to register to vote when they apply for a driver's license if they are at least 18 years of age. It requires states to offer mail-in voter registration too. States must also allow voter registration at state and local offices, including disability and public assistance offices. States must put procedures in place to ensure accurate and up-to-date voter registration lists.

But this step was outdated. The Court decided the problem of suppressed voter rights was no longer a major issue.

Justice Ruth Bader Ginsberg dissented to the *Shelby v. Holder* ruling. She believed it was still necessary for some states to submit election procedures.

The Supreme Court's ruling had a ripple effect across the country. Some states passed election laws that had the potential to restrict voting. In August 2013, North Carolina passed a voter identification law. Critics believed it would suppress the votes of people of color, while supporters believed the law would

CLOSURE OF POLLING PLACES

Election officials nationwide have closed thousands of polling places and reduced staffing and voting hours to cut costs. This has been a problem since the 2013 *Shelby* ruling. A 2018 *USA Today* analysis found that the closure of polling places has had a disproportionate effect on communities of color. Fewer polling places leads to longer lines. This may reduce voter turnout as people cannot take off hours from work to vote. Some people also might not have the means to travel to a distant polling place.

Many states require voters to show some form of ID to an election official to receive a ballot.

In 2016, North Carolina's voter ID law required all voters to show identification at polling places. Student ID cards were not included in the list of acceptable ID forms.

prevent voter fraud. Texas had sought approval for a strict voter identification law in 2012. It had been denied under the Voting Rights Act because of its potential to suppress the vote of low-income people and people of color. But Texas was able to pass the law after the *Shelby* case. Civil rights leaders challenged the law and succeeded in stopping it. A revised version of it went into effect in 2017. North Carolina's law was also challenged. In 2016, a federal judge struck down the law for targeting people of color.

Voting rights organizations increased their efforts to protect voting rights. They filed lawsuits to challenge barriers to voting. These groups organized efforts to support and advance voting rights in local and state jurisdictions. They also increased efforts to register voters and encouraged underrepresented populations to participate in elections.

CONGRESSIONAL, STATE, AND LOCAL ELECTIONS

Voters go to the polls to vote in state and local elections every year. These elections can take place at various times.

They include statewide elections for governors or members of the state legislatures. Cities hold elections for city council members. Voters may also elect judges and other local officials. A popular vote determines the winners of state and local elections.

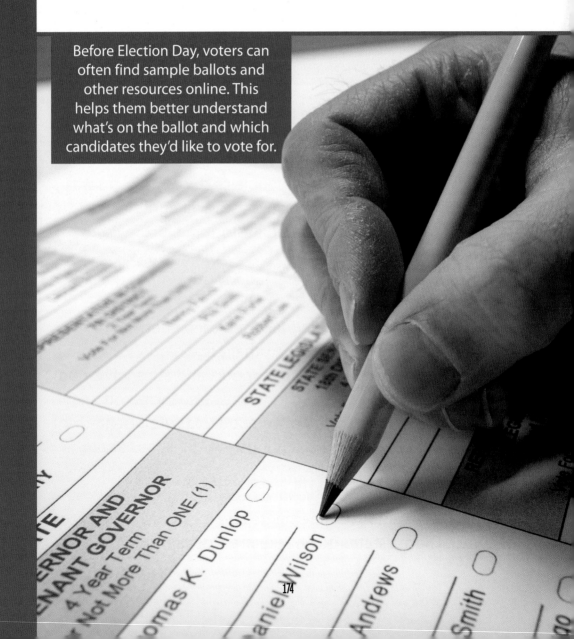

Before Election Day, voters can often find sample ballots and other resources online. This helps them better understand what's on the ballot and which candidates they'd like to vote for.

Public buildings, K–12 schools, and college campuses are common polling stations.

Voters must go to an assigned polling place to cast their ballot in most elections. Polling places are assigned based on where a person lives. Schools and other public facilities are common locations for polling places. A voter's name will be on the roster at his or her assigned polling place. A voter may have to cast a provisional ballot if he or she tries to vote at a different polling place. A provisional ballot is used if questions about a voter's eligibility need to be resolved. The vote may not be counted if the issues are not resolved.

Voter identification requirements vary by state and local jurisdiction. Some states do not require a person to bring a

Primary debates allow voters to learn more about the beliefs of presidential candidates.

voter registration card to the polls. Two-thirds of states require voters to bring a form of identification. The type of identification accepted varies by state. Under federal law, first-time voters who have not registered in person or shown identification previously must show identification to vote.

Voters may vote on a ballot initiative in some states. A ballot initiative is a proposed law that is put on the ballot for the people to consider. The initiative becomes a law if enough people vote for it. As of 2020, 24 states allowed ballot initiatives. Each state has its own rules on how ballot initiatives are handled.

Congressional elections determine a state's representatives in Congress. Senators represent the entire state. Each

member of the House of Representatives represents a specific congressional district within the state. Congressional elections are held every two years. One-third of Senate seats and all House seats are chosen in each congressional election. A popular vote determines the winners of these elections.

PRESIDENTIAL ELECTIONS AND THE ELECTORAL COLLEGE

Candidates running for president first participate in state primary elections and caucuses. Primary elections are often held in the spring. Major political parties use primaries to choose their nominee for the presidential election. The parties hold a national convention after the primaries and caucuses are completed. The parties formally nominate the winning candidates for the general election at the convention.

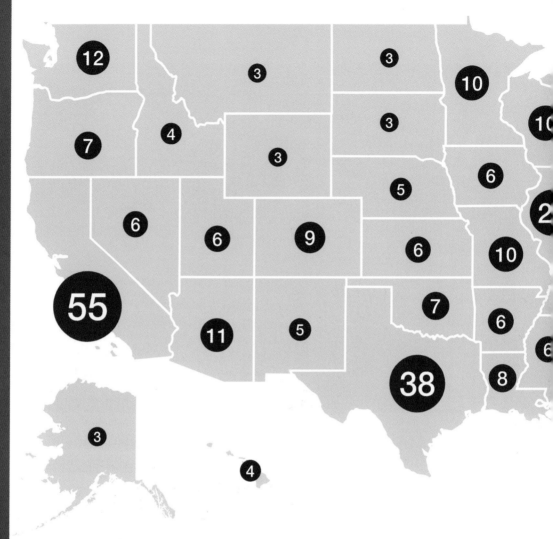

Presidential elections occur every four years on the first Tuesday after the first Monday in November. The process of electing the president and vice president of the United States is slightly different than other elections in the nation. The president and vice president are not directly elected by the popular vote. Instead, they are chosen by electors in the Electoral College. The Electoral College process was described in the Constitution. The Founding Fathers created the Electoral College as a compromise. Some wanted the president directly

States with larger populations have more electoral votes than states with smaller populations. This map shows the electoral votes each state had in the 2020 presidential election.

elected by a popular vote of citizens, and others wanted the president chosen by Congress.

Each state has a number of electors equal to their total representatives in Congress. Washington, DC, has three electors. There are a total of 538 electors. Each state's political parties choose potential electors. But the qualifications for becoming an elector vary by state.

The president selects a running mate to serve as vice president during a presidential election. They run together as a team on the same ballot. Voters cast ballots for their desired candidates. Polling officials tally the votes. In 48 states, the candidate who wins the state's popular vote gets all of the state's electoral college votes. Maine and Nebraska assign their electors proportionally based on the popular vote. A candidate must gather at least 270 votes from electors to win a presidential election.

The presidential winner is typically projected on election night. But the official Electoral College vote occurs in mid-December. At that time electors meet and cast official votes in their states. A state's electors will usually vote for the candidate who won the popular vote in their state. In rare cases, an elector may vote for a different candidate. The Constitution does not require electors to follow their state's popular vote, but some states have this requirement. If an elector violates this requirement, they can be fined, disqualified, or prosecuted.

Over the country's history, some candidates have won the popular vote but lost the Electoral College vote. This situation occurred three times in the 1800s and more recently in 2000 and 2016. No candidate received a majority of electoral votes in 1824. The House of Representatives chooses the president when this happens. The Senate elects the vice president. In 1824, John Quincy Adams was elected president by the House

BUSH V. GORE

Al Gore ran against George W. Bush during the presidential election in 2000. Gore won the popular vote but lost the electoral vote. The day after Election Day, Florida reported that Bush had won its 25 electoral votes. But the margin of victory for the popular vote was less than 0.5 percent. The state did a machine recount of votes. The recount found that Bush was still in the lead. Gore requested a manual recount in four Florida counties. On November 26, Bush was declared the official winner of the state. This led to a series of complaints and recounts. Eventually, the debate about the recounts went to the Supreme Court. The Supreme Court decided that there would be no additional recounts and that Bush would receive Florida's electoral votes.

In 1888, Grover Cleveland, *pictured*, won the popular vote but lost the electoral vote to Benjamin Harrison.

of Representatives. The Senate elected John C. Calhoun as vice president.

ALTERNATE WAYS TO VOTE

There are many reasons why people may not be able to make it to polling places to vote on Election Day. They may have work and family commitments. They may be traveling. Some people have an illness or disability that prevents them from voting in person. Others have difficulty finding transportation to polling places. There are several options for alternate ways

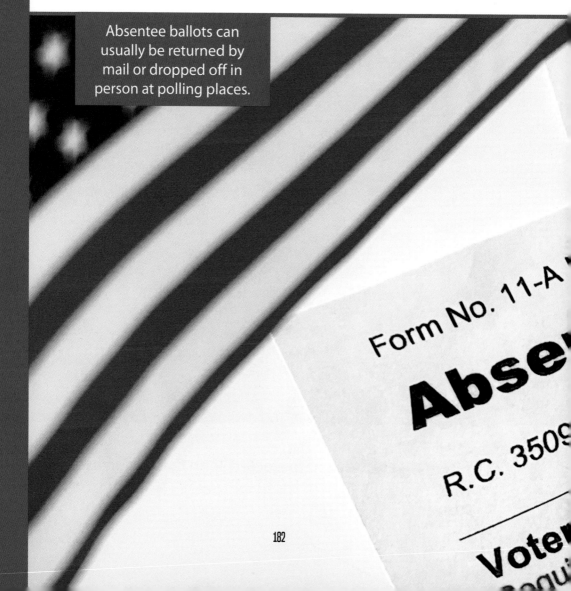

Absentee ballots can usually be returned by mail or dropped off in person at polling places.

Form No. 11-A

Abse

R.C. 3509

Voter

to vote in these cases. People can take steps to make sure their voice is heard when they cannot make it to their polling place.

Every state has absentee voting. This allows a person to vote by mail. Rules on absentee voting vary by state. Some states require an approved reason for absentee voting. These reasons include illness, injury, disability, travel, or being a student at

an out-of-state college or university. Some states also require absentee ballots to be notarized or signed by a witness. Voters should follow their state's instructions on how to request an absentee ballot and the deadlines for returning it. Voters can

Donald Trump raised concerns that mail-in ballots resulted in election fraud in the 2020 election. However, multiple investigations found no evidence of widespread fraud.

OFFICIAL MAIL BALLOT DROP BOX
Caja oficial de deposito para boleta

SAN BERNARDINO COUNTY | Registrar of Voters

OFFICIAL MAIL BALLOT DROP BOX

Caja oficial de deposito para boleta

SBCountyElections.com

SBCountyElections.com

Many states provide secure drop boxes for mail-in ballots.

talk to their state or local election office with any questions about absentee ballots.

Voters can also use mail-in ballots to vote. A mail-in ballot is similar to an absentee ballot, but most states do not require a

Voting allows a citizen's voice to be heard. Even a single vote can make a difference in the outcome of an election.

reason to receive a mail-in ballot. For example, in Pennsylvania, any qualified and registered voter can apply for a mail-in ballot. As with absentee ballots, mail-in ballot rules vary by state.

Voters should check with their state and local election offices with questions.

Many states also permit early voting. Early voting allows registered voters to vote in person on specific dates before Election Day. Early voters do not need to give a reason for voting early. Rules vary by state. State or local election offices can explain how people can participate in early voting.

The right to vote is a responsibility and fundamental right of all US citizens. People have fought for all citizens to have the right and opportunity to vote throughout US history.

Voting in local, state, and federal elections is one way people can make their voices heard and have a say in how the country is governed.

GLOSSARY

bill
A draft of a law presented to a lawmaking body such as Congress.

defendant
A person who has been accused of a crime.

delegate
A representative at a conference or convention.

dissenting
Differing in opinion from the majority.

felony
A serious crime.

jurisdiction
The area in which governing bodies have the authority to exercise their power.

militia
A group of citizens organized for military service.

precedent
A ruling that serves as an example for other rulings.

proportional
Corresponding in size, number, or amount.

prosecution
The legal team that argues the accused person is guilty.

ratify
To approve formally.

resolution
A formal expression of will or intent voted on by an official body or assembled group.

statute
A law passed by the legislative branch of government.

subpoena
To summon a person to appear in court.

suffrage
The right to vote.

tariff
A tax created by the federal government on goods entering or leaving the country.

unanimous
Having complete agreement.

TO LEARN MORE

FURTHER READINGS

Levinson, Cynthia, and Sanford Levinson. *Fault Lines in the Constitution: The Framers, Their Fights, and the Flaws That Affect Us Today*. Peachtree, 2019.

McKinney, Donna B. *The Presidents Encyclopedia*. Abdo, 2023.

Rubin, Susan Goldman. *Give Us the Vote! Over 200 Years of Fighting for the Ballot*. Holiday House, 2020.

ONLINE RESOURCES

Booklinks
NONFICTION NETWORK
FREE! ONLINE NONFICTION RESOURCES

To learn more about the US government, please visit **abdobooklinks.com** or scan this QR code. These links are routinely monitored and updated to provide the most current information available.

INDEX

PHOTO CREDITS

ABDOBOOKS.COM

Published by Abdo Reference, a division of ABDO, PO Box 398166, Minneapolis, Minnesota 55439. Copyright © 2023 by Abdo Consulting Group, Inc. International copyrights reserved in all countries. No part of this book may be reproduced in any form without written permission from the publisher. Encyclopedias™ is a trademark and logo of Abdo Reference.

Printed in the United States of America, North Mankato, Minnesota.
102022
012023

THIS BOOK CONTAINS
RECYCLED MATERIALS

Editor: Angela Lim
Series Designer: Colleen McLaren

LIBRARY OF CONGRESS CONTROL NUMBER: 2022940671

PUBLISHER'S CATALOGING-IN-PUBLICATION DATA

Names: Mooney, Carla, author.
Title: The government encyclopedia / by Carla Mooney
Description: Minneapolis, Minnesota: Abdo Publishing, 2023 | Series: United States encyclopedias | Includes online resources and index.
Identifiers: ISBN 9781098290467 (lib. bdg.) | ISBN 9781098275785 (ebook)
Subjects: LCSH: United States--Juvenile literature. | Politics and government--Juvenile literature. | Federal government--United States--History--Juvenile literature. | Encyclopedias and dictionaries--Juvenile literature.
Classification: DDC 320.973--dc23